HANS W. HANNAU:

THE WEST INDIAN ISLANDS

The West Indian Islands
by Hans W. Hannau

with 90 color photographs and 30 maps

Called the eighth continent, the West Indian Islands are a world of their own, mountainous, exotic, tropical with lush vegetation, an interesting population of varied races, beautiful beaches, romantic bays, colorful villages and towns, historic fortifications, and modern hotels and resorts. They are surrounded by the Atlantic Ocean and the Caribbean Sea, by coral reefs with a brilliantly colorful and unusual marine life, a dream for divers and fishermen. In the forests, in the swamps, and along the coast unique tropical birds create a real adventure for bird watchers.

To catch all this beauty in his masterful color photographs, to describe the interesting history and magnificent scenery and life on these islands is the great achievement of the author, Prof. Hans W. Hannau. He has known these islands intimately for more than a quarter of a century. Starting with pictorial books about single islands, his interest and skill and knowledge has brought him to a major work like this one that describes the whole archipelago of the Caribbean. A delightful and informative book for would-be traveler and nontraveler, it is also a great memento for anybody who has visited the West Indies and will insure his return.

Hans W. Hannau

THE WEST INDIAN ISLANDS
IN FULL COLOR

ARGOS INC.
MIAMI

Maps by **H. Felix Kraus** and **Hedy Eibuschutz**
Endpaper by **Hedy Eibuschutz**

published by **ARGOS Inc.**

ISBN: 0-912458-85-2
Composed in the United States of America
Printed in Spain

INDEX

THE PICTURES

INTRODUCTION

Had there not been a scent of land in the air, the mutinous Spanish sailors on the Pinta, the Niña and the Santa Maria might have forced Columbus to turn back to Spain and to sail into obscurity. But they smelled a special fragrance, saw lovely land birds flying above them, and picked up a fascinating land plant floating on the ocean. They sailed west, to glory.

They landed first on several islands in the Bahamas, and sailed from them to the Caribbean and north coast of Cuba. Columbus described the fertile, temperate and beautiful islands as the "best in the world." The foliage was green, the melody of the birds exquisite and the fragrance of the flowers "the sweetest thing in the world." Since Columbus stepped ashore in the West Indies men and women of many races have found the same special magic in those islands that so enchanted their first European discoverer.

The people who live in and love the Caribbean world today speak Spanish, English, French, Dutch and Portuguese. The dialects compounded from these languages are numerous. The skins of the people who talk these languages range in color from deepest black to albino white. On most of the islands there is equality and harmony among races.

Each of the islands has its own history, culture and tradition. The birds, the plants and the weather also differ among the islands. Some islands lie out of the swing of the seas that are bulldozed high by hurricane winds; some are storm-prone. Some are lush green; a few are arid.

With all their differences, though, the islands are in many ways one world. Geologically, they belong to what was once one land, much of which is now beneath the sea. Many of the high green hills are of ancient volcanic origin. The climate is frost-free, the trade winds silken and caressing. The waters that lap the beaches are always warm, pellucid and beautiful—green in the shallows and Gulf Stream blue in the great depths. But all the islands appeal to the senses. They make people who live there and those who visit happy to be alive, to sense and know the luscious fruits of the land and the sea.

The Spaniards were the first settlers from Europe, but today England has more connections with the islands than any other European nation. The United States, through purchases and treaties, is the second big nation with Caribbean ties. The United States acquired Puerto Rico by treaty after the Spanish-American war, and bought some twenty Virgin islands from Denmark. France is the third most important "outsider," with sovereignty over Martinique, Guadeloupe and other smaller islands. The federated islands of the Netherlands Antilles—Aruba, Bonaire, Curaçao, Saint Maarten, Saba and St. Eustatius—are co-partners with the Kingdom of the Netherlands and have certain autonomous powers within the federation. Haiti, Cuba and the Dominican Republic are independent, free of all European ties.

Today this world throbs with hope. Some of the islands, like Puerto Rico, Aruba and Curaçao, are prosperous and have a high standard of living. Other islands are just coming out of the dark ages, and are experiencing that splendid lift of spirit that comes when people, whose ancestors were enslaved, acquire power and responsibility. Change is in the air, and everywhere the winds say that it is change for the better.

Many of the islands have learned that tourism can be the base for a sound economy. They have seen that tourism can produce jobs for a great many people, a stable economy, healthy growth and attractive home towns for permanent residents. Benefits are reciprocal. Visitors find tropical sun, sand and seas; islands with fascinating histories and the favor of foreign lands. Accommodations for tourists range from luxurious Mediterranean style hotels to quaint beach cottages.

The Caribbean islands are among the world's meccas in the accelerating modern trek toward the sun. Today's visitors find the golden sunshine as valuable as the yellow metal the Spaniards sought. And the vein of sunshine will not run out.

HISTORY

IN THE BEGINNING

The Indians who met Columbus when he landed in the Caribbean were, according to his account, "as naked as when born of their mothers, most handsome men and women." They were so white that if they protected themselves from the sun and air, they would be as white as in Spain." They were Arawak Indians who traded their tame parrots for hawk bells and glass beads. They swam expertly and paddled log canoes across the water. They wove cotton cloth, and from it made hammocks *(hamaca)* which were quickly adopted by the European sailors. Their houses were palmetto thatched shelters and their main foods were a soft corn and fish. The Arawaks had come to the Caribbean islands and the Bahamas from northern South America. Gentle and tractable people, they were to be captured, enslaved and all but exterminated by the Spaniards.

Another people had also preceded the Spaniards to the Antilles. They were the fierce and warlike Caribs. "Carib" means "cannibal" in the Arawak language. Columbus encountered this pugnacious race on his second voyage to the island he called Guadeloupe. In one of their camps he found the remains of a young man being boiled, together with the meat of some parrots and geese. The ferocious Caribs discouraged the Spaniards from settling on the islands they occupied. There are a few Carib Indians still living in Dominica and St. Vincent today.

COLUMBUS SAILS WEST

In 1492 when Columbus took possession of the New World in the name of the King and Queen of Spain, he thought he was claiming the land that produced the spices, silk, gems and gold of the Indies. He expected to meet representatives of the Great Khan of Cathay, for it was to find China that he had sailed west. Instead, he met naked Lucayans, members of the Arawak tribe, gentle and primitive folk whom he called Indians. Some of them had small gold ornaments hanging from holes in their noses.

Columbus called the island on which he landed San Salvador. It is one of the easternmost islands of the Bahamas. The Lucayans indicated that the gold they wore had been found to the south. Columbus sailed in that direction, taking six Lucayans aboard ship so that they might learn Spanish and serve as interpreters.

11

The Spaniards explored the Bahama islands now known as Rum Cay, Long Island, Crooked Island and the tiny cays of the Bahama Bank. The Indians he met told him of two larger islands which they called "Colba" (Cuba) and "Bofio" (Haiti).

On October 28, 1492, Columbus reached the north coast of Cuba. This land he named Juana, in honor of the son of King Ferdinand and Queen Isabella. In this beautiful country the Spaniards found more Indians. Though they searched for evidence of the Oriental civilization of the Great Khan, they found only native villages, with carved wooden statues, domestic dogs and cloth woven from a splendid long-staple cotton. A group of the explorers who made an expedition into the interior of Cuba found natives smoking a grass rolled into tubes which they called "tobacos."

From Cuba the expedition sailed to the north coast of Haiti and anchored in a harbor Columbus named Mole-St. Nicholas. St. Nicholas was a pope who had forbidden conversion by force and reproved cruelty to pagans. The harbor has the same name today. This island Columbus also claimed for Spain and named La Isla Española. Today it is called Hispaniola and includes both Haiti and the Dominican Republic.

In Haiti the explorers met a king, called "cacique" by the Indians. Columbus and the king dined together and traded Indian gold for Spanish bedspreads, amber beads and orange-flower water. On Christmas day of 1492 the Santa Maria went aground on the island of Hispaniola. Columbus and his men built a fort on the island. Today the coast of Hispaniola is much the same as when Columbus first described it. There are no more Arawaks, however. Black descendants of Africans are the natives who live along the beaches.

Columbus returned to Spain aboard the Niña, accompanied by the Pinta. The glowing accounts he gave of the islands resulted in seventeen ships setting forth with him on his second voyage to colonize the New World. He had recognized the pattern of the westerly trade winds and made the Atlantic crossing in twenty-one days. When he arrived at the settlement of Navidad on the northern coast of Hispaniola, he found it destroyed. He established a second colony, Isabella, on the same shore. From Isabella he went on to the south coast of Cuba, and then to Jamaica, still searching for Marco Polo's Cathay.

The Spanish colonists succeeded in provoking the Indians to war, and in 1496 Columbus' brother Bartholomé led the Spaniards to the south coast of Hispaniola. There he founded Santo Domingo, the city that was to be the capital of the Spanish Indies for the next fifty years.

Columbus' third voyage in 1498 did not end happily. With a few volunteers Columbus discovered and explored Trinidad and made his first landfall on the continent of South America. But when he reached Santo Domingo, he found mutiny in progress. Two ships were sent back to Spain to report the rebellion. In the meanwhile malcontents had reported Columbus was a tyrant and Francisco de Bodadilla was sent from Spain to investigate. Although Columbus had succeeded in stopping the rebellion, in October, 1500, he was sent with his brother back to Spain under arrest.

Columbus was eventually exonerated by the King and Queen, and outfitted for a fourth voyage in 1502. His landfall in the Caribbean was Martinique. He rode out a hurricane off Hispaniola, anchored off Honduras and explored the coasts of Nicaragua, Costa Rica and Panama. He returned to Spain in 1504. His twelve years in the Caribbean had made him a rich man. He died in 1506. He had wished to be buried in Hispaniola, and in 1536 his body was removed from Spain and buried in the Cathedral at Santo Domingo.

THE ERA OF SPANISH RULE

Santo Domingo remained the most important settlement in the Spanish Caribbean, and it grew rapidly. Gold was mined for two decades, though no great vein of treasure was found. Oranges, figs, lemons and bananas were introduced. Pigs and herds of wild cattle thrived, and hides and tallow were exported to Spain. Sugar, which was to shape the fate of the Caribbean for centuries, was introduced and the first sugar mill was built in Hispaniola in 1508. Sugar requires much unskilled labor for its cutting, and it must be milled as soon as it is cut. This led to attempts to enslave the Indians of the Caribbean and the Bahamas, but they fought or committed suicide. Blacks were brought from West Africa as slaves.

Jamaica was first settled by the Spanish in 1509, but Spain never considered the island important. It yielded no gold and was given over largely to cattle ranches in Spanish times.

Settlement of Cuba began in 1511 under the leadership of the energetic Diego Velazquez, a strict disciplinarian who launched the project as a private investment. Within three years his small force controlled the island, and in the first five years as governor he founded seven towns. The first was Santiago, the chief settlement until ships heading home to Spain by way of Florida channel north of Cuba brought Havana to the forefront.

With Balboa's discovery of the Isthmus of Panama and the Pacific coast in 1513, and Cortes' conquest of Mexico in 1519, the Caribbean islands became the highroad to the rich empire of which Spain had dreamed. For the first decades after Columbus' discovery, other European nations had paid little attention to Spain's colonies. When the Spanish ships began returning home laden with gold and silver, however, bold spirits from France, Holland and England began to descend upon the shipping. Spain attempted to control the import of goods from Europe to the Caribbean, but smugglers of slaves and other necessities thrived by under-selling the Spaniards.

Cattle-raising was originally the predominant source of income for the Spanish settlers, but sugar eventually became the major export. The demand was high in Europe for sugar, and as the investments in mills and slaves from West Africa increased, the exports increased.

THE CHALLENGES TO SPAIN

The English made their first settlement in the Caribbean in 1623 at St. Kitts in the Leeward Islands. Dutch traders took over several small islands—Aruba, Bonaire, Curaçao, Saba, St. Maarten and St. Eustatius—between 1630 and 1640: Today these islands are the Netherlands Antilles. The Dutch wanted them as bases for trade and fighting. When they were not fighting, they brought slaves out to the islands and took sugar and tobacco back home.

The French, not to be outdone, arrived not long after the English settled St. Kitts and also established a colony on that island. Martinique and Guadeloupe became French colonies in 1635. Saint-Domingue on Hispaniola was also settled by the French.

The English claimed Barbados (1624 or 1625) and in 1632 settled in Antigua and Montserrat. The English and Dutch jointly tried to settle the Virgin Islands at St. Croix about 1625. Britain went to war with Spain over Jamaica and took the island from the Spaniards in 1655. It is curious to note that in the 1640s the British white population in the West Indies peaked and since then has declined.

Competition for trade with the West Indies spurred on wars in Europe. England went to war against Spain and France many times between 1739 and 1763. Sugar from the colonies sparked the war between England and France in 1744. The attacks of each side on the other's colonies were simply an effort to put the competitor out of the business of producing sugar.

English and French rivalry flared into the Seven Years War in 1756. Spain came into that war in 1762, and an English fleet took Havana in the West Indies and Manila in the Pacific. England emerged victorious, but had to return some of the colonies that had been taken in order to get France and Spain to agree to a peace treaty. Many Englishmen argued that England should keep Guadeloupe in preference to Canada. However, in the end England received the whole continent of North America east of the Mississippi as settlement, including Canada and Florida. Martinique and Guadeloupe were returned to France and Cuba to Spain.

With the Peace of Paris, a great age dawned for the French West Indies. For three decades, until the French Revolution, the French colonies took the lead over the English in exporting sugar. The French sold their sugar, molasses and rum cheaper than the English, and this encouraged a brisk trade with the British colonies in North America. New England traders sold grain, salt fish, timber and horses to the French. Jamaica, Barbados and the British Leeward islands had passed their peak of sugar prosperity. Free ports had been established by the Dutch at St. Eustatius and Curaçao. After the war, the French developed a free port system on Martinique, Guadeloupe, St. Lucia and Saint-Domingue.

The American Revolution brought war and heavy taxes to the English islands. The English colonists in the British West Indies remained loyal to England. France got into the fighting in 1778 and Spain in 1779. The French captured Dominica, St. Vincent and Grenada. The Dutch recognized the independence of the United States in 1780, and helped the newborn nation with a brisk trade in munitions. In retaliation, the British West Indian fleet took over St. Eustatius and devastated the island. When all the Caribbean fighting was over, Tobago changed hands once again and was ceded to France. Florida became a Spanish possession.

THE POWDER KEG EXPLODES

Sugar was in some ways the curse of the Caribbean. The industry brought economic, political and social upheaval to the islands, much of it violent and destructive.

The Spaniards brought the first African slaves to the Caribbean in 1510 to work their mines and sugar plantations on Hispaniola. They came from West Africa. Factories were set up along the Guinea coast where African chiefs and kings brought slaves for trade. Each chief or king received a fee for each slave sold, plus a commission. First the Portuguese, then the English, Dutch and French came to fill the growing demand for the Caribbean plantations. When the trade began, a good horse would buy fifteen slaves. Later, the Africans demanded payment in their own coin, cowrie shells and certain European goods.

The Middle Passage taken by the slave ships across the Atlantic was pure hell. The slaves were crowded together in the hold, swept by small-pox and dysentery. It is conservatively estimated that six per cent of all slaves shipped during the centuries that slave trade flourished died on the Atlantic voyage.

Buyers of this human cargo in the West Indies had preferences as to tribes. The Gold Coast Negroes, the Koromantyn, were tough, hard-working, brave and stubborn. From them were to come leaders of slave rebellions. From the tribes to the north and east of Sierra Leone came Mohammedan Negroes who could read and write in Arabic. They were not fitted for hard labor in the fields. Papaws from Whydah were popular as slaves because they worked hard, were skilled farmers, and were afraid of death and, consequently, submitted to discipline. The yellowish-colored Eboes from the Bight of Benin were timid and despondent, given to suicide, though they were cannibals at home. Negroes from Angola and the Congo were considered excellent mechanics, better fitted for domestic service than for work in the fields.

When the slaves were sold from ships or wharfs, every effort was made to break up friendships, families and any links with their past. The planter gave his slave, who arrived naked, a shirt, trousers, a knife, a hat and a handkerchief. For the first few months after arrival, they were "seasoned" or left to adjust to the new country and the new climate.

Almost from the beginning, maroons (escaped slaves who had fled to the bush) were found on most of the major islands. In Jamaica they joined native Indians who had fled to the hills.

The brutal institution of slavery began to decline at about the time of the French Revolution. Talk of the "Rights of Man" raised whirlwinds of emotion in the Caribbean. White planters on French Saint-Domingue (now Haiti) demanded the rights to do what they pleased on the island. The slaves revolted and soon bloodshed bathed the island, with mulattoes fighting whites and blacks fighting mulattoes as well as whites. The revolutionary Jacobin party ruled in France and sent an army to enforce liberty, equality and fraternity. They fought on the side of the revolutionary slaves and proclaimed a conditional emancipation in August 1793. The French National Assembly confirmed the ruling and whites fled the island.

England and Spain went to war against revolutionary France, and England sent an expedition against Saint-Domingue, partly in fear that the slave rebellion would spread. Spread it did. The second maroon war broke out in Jamaica in 1795. The British were driven from Saint-Domingue by the military skill of Pierre Dominique

Toussaint, "L'Ouverture," first of a remarkable series of black Haitian military leaders. When war broke out between France and Spain, Toussaint raised an army of some four thousand black troops and fought the French. When the English invaded, he feared the restoration of slavery, turned against the Spaniards and fought on the side of the French Republican army. The United States sent him ships and supplies to fight the English. In 1801 he drew up a constitution for the island and named himself governor-general for life. Napoleon would not tolerate this and sent troops to the island to capture the black hero. Toussaint died in a French prison.

The blacks of the island had lost their first great leader, but never again were they to be subject to alien domination. An African-born slave, Jean Jacque Dessalines, took over as head of the forces Toussaint had led. In 1804 he changed the name of Saint-Domingue to Haiti, which means "mountainous" in the Taino Indian language. In the same year he proclaimed himself Emperor of Haiti. After Dessalines' death in 1806, the giant Negro Henri Christophe ruled the land until his death in 1820. The southern part of Haiti was dominated by Pétion, a mulatto leader.

After the revolt of maroons and the slaves in Jamaica in 1795, the European nations could see the course they must take. Between 1804 and 1820 slave trade was abolished by Denmark, Holland, Spain and Sweden. Cuba continued to import slaves until 1865. Slaves rebelled in Barbados and again and again in Jamaica. Slavery was finally abolished in the British West Indies in 1833 and in the French colonies in 1848.

Cuba, the most cultured and prosperous of the Spanish colonies, was the last of the larger islands to ban slavery. It had a thriving economy based on sugar cane, tobacco and pig farming, all of which needed a continual import of slaves. The white minority on the island encouraged immigration from Europe and a strong, articulate, liberal element began to grow among the white Cubans. The slave trade, banned in 1817, was finally halted in 1865. Not until 1880 were provisions made for the emancipation of slaves, and in 1886 they were finally freed.

During the nineteenth century Britain tried numerous techniques of governing her West Indian colonies. Emancipation brought about wide social and political change. Three-quarters of a million people with no experience in the responsibilities of self-government or even in the planning of their own lives were set free. Landowners became absentees. There were uprisings. Crown colony government replaced the old representative system on most of the British islands. This type of government was relatively impartial and, to a degree, paternal, and introduced needed economic development to the colonies. This interim period lasted until after World

War I when the black people began to stir again with a hunger for more independence and responsibility.

After slavery was ended in the French islands, France took the wise, bold policy of integrating the colonies more closely with home, giving the islanders the freedom all Frenchmen enjoyed. Martinique, Guadeloupe and Cayenne each elected representatives to the National Assembly. For more than a century they have remained strongly tied to France. French in culture, government and politics.

FREEDOM COMES

Spain's power had waned toward the end of the nineteenth century and there were only three Spanish colonies in the West Indies—Cuba, Santo Domingo and Puerto Rico. When the slaves rose in French Saint-Domingue, they also raided across the border into Spanish Santo Domingo, a sleepy land given largely to cattle raising. Haiti ruled Santo Domingo until 1844 and hard feelings between the two lands of that island still occasionally erupt. The Haitians were expelled in 1844, and mulattoes ruled a new Dominican Republic until 1861, when Spain reoccupied that portion of Hispaniola. The land was so poor Spain promptly withdrew. Anarchy and tyranny followed. For eighteen years Ulises Heureaux was dictator. When he was assassinated in 1899 the country was bankrupt and chaos reigned.

Cuba in the nineteenth century experienced growth and change quite different from that of its neighboring islands. It was the largest and richest of the islands and had a prideful heritage and many well-educated citizens. White immigrants continued to arrive from Spain as political disorganization mounted in the mother country. Sugar production went up. The best tobacco in the world was grown on small Cuban farms, and the people had the skill that is required to cure fine tobacco. Disgusted with Spain's incompetence, white creoles in Cuba began to agitate for freedom. Spain sent out militarists to suppress the freedom-fever. Slaves revolted. The United States in 1848 offered to buy Cuba from Spain, but the offer was declined.

One of the great heroes of the Caribbean in the nineteenth century was Carlos Manuel de Cespédes, a liberal Cuban land-owner and lawyer. A junta of Cuban exiles in New York formed to support him. Cespédes declared Cuban independence at Yara in 1868. The Ten Years War that followed was distinguished more by courage than by organization, and consisted principally of bitter guerilla fighting in the hills. Liberal spirits in the United States made gun-running and filibustering expeditions to Cuba, carrying weapons to the rebels in this war. In one such expedition fifty-three members of the crew of a U.S. ship were court-martialed and shot by

18

their Spanish captors. Cespédes was killed in a Spanish raid. The fighting lasted ten years because Spain was in the throes of internal strife, the Carlist War. The insurgents surrendered in 1878. Slaves were emancipated in Cuba between 1880 and 1886.

The peace that followed until 1895 was uneasy. Conditions on the island were hurt even more by the American Sugar Refining Company, a United States corporation created in 1890. The company, which became known as the "Sugar Trust," controlled prices of Cuban sugar, and the prices dropped. The McKinley Tariff on sugar and tobacco imported into the U.S. also was a blow to the Cuban economy.

In 1895 another magnetic leader led a successful revolt. José Martí was both dedicated and able, and he led the Cuban junta. In the war that followed there were atrocities on both sides. Following the sinking of the battleship Maine by an explosion on a "courtesy" visit to Havana, the United States went to war against Spain. After Spain's defeat, the U.S. annexed Puerto Rico and obtained a naval base at Guantánamo in Cuba.

Today La Republica De Cuba, most populous island of the Caribbean, is a democratic socialist republic, and since 1958 has been working out its destiny under Fidel Castro. Major emphasis has been placed by the government on the development of agriculture. Oil was discovered in the 1950s. Numerous cement factories have expanded. Sugar, tobacco and minerals are still principal exports of the island.

Puerto Rico was a sleepy island when it was annexed by the United States in 1898. Fierce Caribs had initially discouraged Spanish settlement, and for centuries it had been one of the poorest Spanish colonies. Poor and backward it remained until after World War II. Under the leadership of Luis Muñoz Marín, a progressive program to lure tourists, industry and investment was launched. Today the island vibrates with pride and progress. Puerto Rico became the first overseas commonwealth territory of the United States on July 3, 1950, when President Truman signed legislation giving Puerto Ricans power to write their own constitution and assume greater control of internal affairs. As a territory, the island has enjoyed a rising standard of living and does not have to pay federal income taxes. There is a movement for independence, but in a plebiscite in 1967 an overwhelming majority of voters voted to retain their present relationship with the United States.

The twentieth century has brought enviable happiness and prosperity to the Netherlands Antilles—Aruba, Bonair, Curaçao, Saba, St. Maarten and St. Eustatius. General suffrage and a new constitution were introduced in 1948, and on December 15, 1954, the Netherlands Antilles became an equal and autonomous co-partner in the Kingdom of the Netherlands. Two of the world's largest oil refineries are located on Curaçao and Aruba. For more than a decade these bright and beautiful

Dutch islands have been attracting tourists with great success, and increasing numbers of visitors enjoy modern, luxurious and hospitable resorts.

Guadeloupe, Martinique and Cayenne form an Overseas Department of the Republic of France, a status attained on March 19, 1946. The Department has the right to appoint three deputies to the National Assembly, two members of the Senate and it is represented on the French Economic and Social Council. The economy of the islands is largely agricultural, and education is free and compulsory from six to sixteen years of age. Attractive resorts and epicurean restaurants supplement the fine beaches and the magnificent scenery of the islands as tourist attractions.

After economic unrest and riots in the 1930s, the British colonies in the Caribbean took the road to freedom. On Jamaica and Trinidad, the largest of these islands, universal adult suffrage was introduced under constitutions in 1944. They attained independence in 1962, and are members of the British Commonwealth of Nations. They joined the Organization of American States (OAS) in June, 1969. Both are also members of the United Nations and Caribbean Free Trade Associations. Trinidad and Tobago are united under one government.

Most of the smaller islands that were formerly colonies of Great Britain, such as Antigua, obtained new constitutions leading to self-governing status in 1966 and are now States in Association with the United Kingdom, with full internal self-government. Other small islands, such as Montserrat and the Cayman Islands, are still British colonies. There, after negotiation conducted during 1966, the islanders elected not to move into the status of self-government.

Today these islands are new frontiers, where pioneers are learning to trust their own strength, courage and good sense. They are mastering the arts of politics and hospitality. The alluring fragrance of new-found freedom is being carried by the trade winds across the green peaks and white beaches. There is a special lilt of life on these islands.

HENRY MORGAN

PIRATES

OF THE SPANISH MAIN

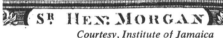

Like hawks they swooped about the Caribbean for three centuries, the pirates who enriched the beautiful region with legends of treasures. In myth they are dashing and bold but in fact, many were cruel, dirty villains.

Plundering upon the sea in the New World began almost as soon as the lumbering Spanish galleons began carrying gold, silver and emeralds back to Spain. The great gold treasures of the Americas were found in four mining centers—two in Mexico, one in Peru, and one, the fabled Potosí mine, in Bolivia. The Pope had divided the non-Christian world between Spain and Portugal. Portugal was given Africa with its fortune in slaving. Spain was given the western world with its riches in gold. The Protestant nations of Europe did not recognize the legality of this partition of the globe.

Privateers and pirates began to swarm to the Caribbean. Privateers only attacked and plundered their country's enemies. They fitted out their ships at their own expense, were granted letters of marque by their kings and queens, and shared their loot with the crown. Pirates attacked anyone, and were men without allegiance to any nation.

First of these sea-raiders were the French corsairs who began to raid the Spanish galleons when Francis I was king. Before he was beheaded by the Spanish, Jean Florin confessed that he had robbed and sunk one hundred and fifty Spanish ships. In 1555 Captain François le Clerk, "Pegleg," led French corsairs who sacked Havana and held the rich for ransom.

John Hawkins was initially a slave smuggler and a privateer, one of the first of those encouraged by Queen Elizabeth when she came to the English throne in 1558. She knighted him, as she did Sir Francis Drake who began his career as the captain of one of Hawkins' small ships. Drake sailed in glory when he went raiding Her Majesty's enemies around the world from 1577 to 1580. Victorious in raids on Santo Domingo, Havana, Cartagena, Panama and St. Augustine in Florida, Drake never considered himself reprehensible. His fighting was against England's foes.

"The Brotherhood of the Coast" was the name of that group of buccaneers who camped on the western end of Hispaniola. They dried strips of meat by smoking them over a slow fire called "boucan," and thence the name "buccaneers." They were shipwrecked sailors, deserters, criminals, adventurers, free spirits. From the buccaneers, pirate crews were recruited.

Tortuga, an island just north of Hispaniola, was an early haunt of international buccaneers in the seventeenth century. English buccaneers headquartered at Port Royal in Jamaica with the approval of Jamaica's governors. From this stronghold Henry Morgan sacked the Spanish Main. He died in 1688 as lieutenant-governor of Jamaica. Port Royal perished in an earthquake in 1692 when it sank beneath the sea.

Captain William Kidd was a respected ship captain in New York when he was sent by England to wipe out pirates in the Indian Ocean. He turned pirate himself and looted ships from the East Indies to the Caribbean. His infamy lived on long after he was captured and hanged in London in 1701.

Another of the more famous pirates was Edward Teach, called Blackbeard. He was a huge, fierce man with a black beard that reached almost to his waist. Blackbeard's hideaway was in St. Thomas in the Virgin Islands, until he began to headquarter on New Providence Island in the Bahamas. It was purported that he had an alliance with Governor Charles Eden of North Carolina. Teach was killed off the Outer Banks of North Carolina by Lieutenant Robert Maynard of the Royal Navy.

The honor of sweeping the last of the Caribbean pirates from the sea goes to the United States Navy under the command of Commodore David Porter in the 1820s. With England's aid and an appropriation from Congress of $500,000, Porter outfitted his squadron. He captured scores of pirate ships from his base in Key West and by 1830 the Jolly Roger flew no more.

THE PEOPLE OF THE CARIBBEAN

Throughout the islands today there is an exciting mixture of different ethnic strains from all over the world—African, European, Oriental, Indian. The original natives, Arawaks and Caribs, were all but exterminated. Aruba is one of the few islands on which a sizeable Indian population remained for some centuries after white men arrived. There the high cheekbones, the straight black hair and the friendliness of the Arawaks can be seen in many hospitable Arubans. In most of the islands the black people who were brought in chains from Africa are in the majority, and they are inheriting that beautiful earth.

There is a great deal of difference among the black people. Many islanders, of course, have considerable white blood. But among the Africans who seem to have undiluted Negro ancestry there are distinct differences in face and physique. This is not surprising, since Africa is a land of many different and distinct tribes, from the Mohammedan Negroes in the north of the continent, with their silky hair and aquiline features, to the powerful big, black men from the Congo.

Attitudes of masters toward their slaves shaped the future that is being born today. Many freed their illegitimate offspring, children of their slaves. Slaves could also, under Spanish law, buy their freedom or win it by saving their master's life. Almost from the beginning there were a number of free Negroes and many free mulattoes. They formed a separate caste or class, above the Negro slaves, below the white slave-owner. White blood, as evidenced by light brown color, was more desirable than black.

Today, on many of the newly independent islands, this is not true. In some parts of the Caribbean it is easier for a black man to get a job or hold a political post than it is for a mulatto, and far easier than it is for a white man. This is particularly true in the islands that once were English colonies, for the English considered their slaves property, not people. They drew a line that shut blacks out of their world, and now white men are leaving Jamaica and Trinidad, as a line shutting them out of the dominant black world is being drawn.

The French were different. French soldiers fought beside black slaves against white slave-owners in Saint Domingue during the French Revolution. The women of Martinique, white and black, for some centuries have been famous for their beauty.

The easiest race relations, over the centuries, have developed between blacks and whites in what were once Spanish colonies, because the Spanish were the most humane. In the islands where the Spanish influence dominated, color lines were not drawn so sharply and arbitrarily. There is a mixing, and an easier, more equal, feeling among people of all colors.

The Africans who were brought to the New World did not retain their languages. They learned English, Spanish, French or Dutch. Whole new languages were developed, like the Papiamento of Aruba and Curaçao, which is a mixture of Spanish, Portuguese and Dutch, with some Arawak and English words. The slaves brought a musical lilt in their speech, which they gave to the languages they adopted. They brought their gods of Africa, and their magic, Obeah, which still lives throughout the Caribbean. Many still believe as devoutly in the witch-doctors who treat them as in the churches they may attend. They brought voodoo, which is still practiced in Haiti.

When the slave trade ended, the plantation owners were desperate for labor, many East Indians and Chinese came to the Caribbean in the last century to work as indentured laborers on five-years contracts. A considerable number of Chinese coolies were brought into Cuba. Many stayed. The Chinese became shopkeepers. It is not unusual to see Oriental features in boys and girls born in the Antilles.

Along with freedom and the right to govern themselves, the people of the Caribbean have also acquired the responsibility for their own economy. This has resulted in a major new industry—tourism—that has supplanted sugar cane on many of the islands. Puerto Rico and Jamaica set the pace after World War II. Sunseekers from North and South America and Europe began to flock to this beautiful world. Resort hotels and attractive accommodations were built. The people could see that tourism produced more jobs than other major industries. Learning the arts of professional hospitality has come easy to Caribbean islanders, because they are by nature a fun-loving people with a positive preference for happiness.

All through the islands new resorts are being built. Yachtsmen find new hideaways, adventurers come back with tales of beautiful beaches and exotic rain forests. Though the black people who are in the majority draw the line at letting white people run their world, they are gracious and easy-going with their guests. There is a spontaneous, whole-hearted joy of life that pervades this world, even though living may often be bitterly hard and the people poor.

PUERTO RICO

Puerto Rico is a place where people love to live because it has fine mountains, a warm, crystal-clear sea, spectacular beauty and a kind climate. However, for centuries after it was discovered in 1493, the island was poor and life hard for most people. Juan Ponce de León settled this land in 1508. It was a possession of Spain until the Spanish-American War. Puerto Rico became a United States territory under the Treaty of Paris in 1899.

For decades thereafter the island was poor. Today Puerto Rico is an inspiration to the other Antillean islands, thanks to Operation Bootstrap, an inspiration of former Governor Muñoz Marín. He once said, "We must live like angels and produce like devils." He designed a program to court industry and tourists that has been wondrously successful. Tax advantages have lured more than five hundred new industries, which range from small textile plants to a huge Union Carbide plant. The tourist industry is ever-expanding.

Puerto Rico is one hundred miles long and forty miles wide. The most easterly of the larger islands of the West Indies, it rises beside the waters of the Brownson Deep, which go down 27,000 feet below the surface. The highest mountain peak, Cerro de Punta in the central part of the island, rises to 4,398 feet. The climate is practically perfect, for the island is far enough north to escape oppresive tropical heat, and the trade winds cool the land. There are miles of fine beaches, wide fertile plains and splendid forests filled with ferns and flowers, such as the Caribbean National Forest on the slopes of Luquillo Mountains.

25

Ponce de León gave the island its name, which literally means rich or beautiful port. San Juan is the capital city. The warring European powers—Spain, France, England, and Holland—fought over Puerto Rico from time to time. Massive fortresses were built by the Spanish to protect the harbor. Luis Muñoz Rivera, Puerto Rico's George Washington, won dominion status for the island from Spain in 1897. Two years later Puerto Rico became the first "colony" of the United States. The islanders became American citizens in 1917, and they voted to establish the self-governing Commonwealth of Puerto Rico in 1952.

San Juan is an enchanting city. The Old City is Spanish colonial in style, with great forts and narrow streets. Built on an island, it is today linked by causeway and by bridges to the mainland. Under the Old City is a network of tunnels that once linked strategic places, but it is now closed.

In the Old City of San Juan the historical landmarks include Castillo de San Felipe del Morro. Completed in 1586, this fort covers more than two hundred acres. The Fortaleza was rebuilt in 1640, and is half-fort, half-palace. Today it is the official residence of the Governor of Puerto Rico. Near the seaside gardens of this beautiful estate is the Cathedral of St. John the Baptist, where the bones of Ponce de León lie. One of the oldest churches in the Western Hemisphere is the Church of San José, built in 1523. A bronze statue of Ponce de León forged from captured cannons dominates the Plaza nearby.

Other places to visit in the Old City are the Casa Blanca, which was built as a home for Ponce de León in 1523, and El Convento, a seventeenth century convent for Carmelite nuns which has been converted into an attractive hotel. Another massive fortress, San Cristóbal, commands the eastern approaches to the harbor.

There is also much that is new and attractive in and around San Juan. The horse race track, Hipódromo de El Comandante, is one of the prettiest in the world. A pleasure park beside the sea, Parque Muñoz Rivera, overlooks a baseball stadium. The stately Capitol, the Supreme Court building, the University of Puerto Rico at Río Piedras are all handsome and interesting modern buildings.

Sightseeing is pleasant in Puerto Rico, not only because the sights are so beautiful but also because the island has more than three thousand miles of excellent roads. The Condado section on the outskirts of San Juan has the luxurious resort hotels. Palm-shaded Luquillo Beach is one of the most beautiful in the Caribbean. El Yunque, the tropical rain forest that is the Caribbean National Forest, is on a mountain slope less than an hour's drive from San Juan.

Ponce, the second largest city on the island, offers many pleasures. Colonial Spain is quite as much in evidence as in San Juan, but in a different style. Here there are colonial mansions, romantic walled patios, balconies overlooking flowering gardens.

Seventeenth-century view of San Juan. (1671)   *Casa Del Libro, San Juan*

A red and black striped building was once the Ponce firehouse. The Cathedral of Our Lady of Guadaloupe is serene. This city, with its two lovely plazas, proves that the Spaniards had a fine sense of how to design a city for human pleasure. Today luxurious resort hotels in Ponce offer all the amenities to tourists. Outstanding is the Ponce Museum of Art, a modern building with an excellent collection of paintings.

On the western tip of Puerto Rico is Mayagüez, which is the island's third largest city. Here an agricultural experiment station is said to have the largest collection of tropical plants in the Western Hemisphere. This is an important port city. Artists with needle and thread have made Mayagüez famous for embroidery and needlework.

A drive along the coast leads to La Parguera and "The Bay of Living Light." The phosphorescence in the waters at night is almost bright enough to read by. Continuing north is the ancient town of San German. Founded by Diego Columbus, here the Porta Coeli Church was built in 1513.

"Portorriqueños," as the islanders call themselves, are a musical people. Great musical artists of the world appear at the three-week musical festival held in the spring. It has been shaped around the gifted cellist Pablo Casals. The islanders and their visitors also enjoy symphony concerts, opera, ballet and theater.

Visitors to Puerto Rico need never be at a loss for things to do. Night-life is fascinating and sophisticated, with entertainment, gambling casinos, fine restaurants and dancing. During the day, deepsea fishing, shore fishing and lake fishing reward anglers. There are facilities for all sorts of water sports; water skiing, skin-diving and sailing. Golfers have many choices among excellent courses. Puerto Rico is a rich port, indeed.

27

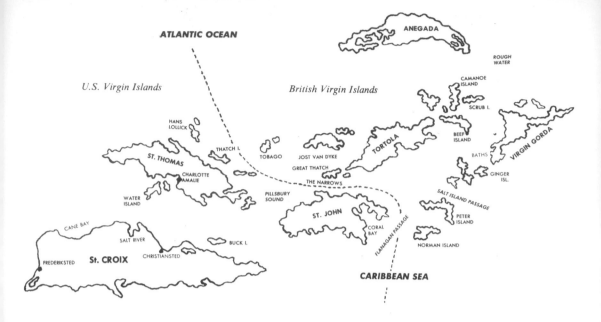

THE VIRGIN ISLANDS

A group of jagged rocks on the horizon covered with spray and mist like wisps of veils, reminded Columbus of a giant frieze of kneeling women. He thought of St. Ursula and her eleven thousand virgins awaiting martyrdom and he called the rocky islands the Virgins. These volcanic cones, inactive for millennia, loom to heights of 1,500 feet above the sea. They are located just east of Puerto Rico on the rim of the Antilles beside the Atlantic. They include three small islands, St. Thomas, St. Croix and St. John, and some forty-eight smaller islands and cays.

The history of the Virgins is unique. These islands were the northernmost reached by the Caribs. The Spanish never settled them successfully. The Dutch tried and failed in the seventeenth century. It was Denmark that first successfully occupied these jewels of the sea, and Christian V took possession in 1671.

The three larger islands remained Danish until World War I. Then the United States, with a need for Caribbean bases, bought them from the Danes. The smaller British Virgin Islands lie to the east of St. John. They have been English since 1672, and Tortola is the largest of the Virgins in the British colony. The U. S. Virgins, which include many small islands as well as the three larger ones, have the status of an organized by unincorporated territory and are under the jurisdiction of the U. S. Department of the Interior. Residents of the islands are U. S. citizens but do not vote in U. S. presidential elections. They elect their unicameral legislature.

THE U.S. VIRGIN ISLANDS

ST. THOMAS

St. Thomas, second largest, of the Virgins, is the mecca for most tourists among these islands. It has a delightful style. The capital city is Charlotte Amalie, which has an excellent deep-water harbor. Behind the pastel town, redolent of the eighteenth century, is the mountain range that cuts St. Thomas in two.

Swimming, sailing, strolling, shopping and delving into a sweet past draw an ever-increasing tide of island-lovers to St. Thomas. Charlotte Amalie's shopping center is as fascinating as Istanbul's bazaar. The shops are built in what were once terra cotta warehouses. Splendid arches of brick and stone and floors laid with Italian tiles and Spanish marble have been uncovered. Here is sold the exquisite imported merchandise from all over the world that makes this one of the most cherished free-port shopping districts in the Caribbean.

Old Fort Christian in St. Thomas has, over the past three hundred years, been a jail, courthouse, Governor's residence, police station and again a prison. It is a picturesque structure, where they once hanged pirates. Other interesting sights on the island include the Nisky Moravian Mission and the tower of Bluebeard's Castle. The second oldest synagogue in the New World is on St. Thomas.

No waters in the world are better for fishing, sailing and scuba diving than those of St. Thomas. A wide range of delightful hotels continue to expand as new visitors fall in love with this jewel of the Caribbean.

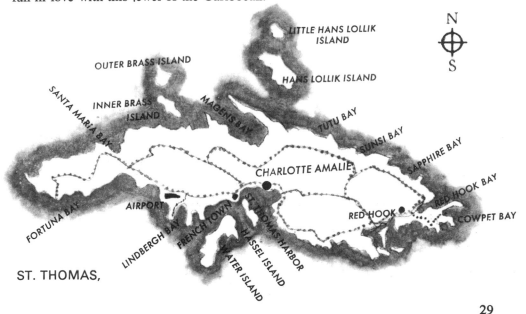

29

ST. CROIX

Whereas St. Thomas is a gregarious all-embracing island, St. Croix is exclusive and quiet. It invites those who love to think of themselves as plantation owners, or lords and ladies of the manorial eighteenth century. St. Croix, the largest of the U.S. Virgins, is twenty-eight miles long and about ten miles wide.

Christiansted, the minute, red-roofed capital of the island, is a scene from an Isak Dinesen story of eighteenth century Danish privateers in the Caribbean. Pastel colored buildings give this port city part of its charm, as do the flaming royal poinciana trees, hibiscus and bougainvillea vines. A seventeenth century Dutch fort, Fort Christiansvaern, is a sight of the city, as are its old churches and stores.

Frederiksted is another quaint town on St. Croix. Because of a fire in 1878, its architecture is Victorian in flavor. There are many large estates on the island with names that are evocative of their merry past: Anna's Hope, Good Hope, Upper Love, Lower Love, Jealousy, Sally's Fancy, Judith's Fancy.

The wave of tourists that has fallen under the spell of the Virgins is washing over St. Croix. Fine resorts, hotels, inns and lodgings have burgeoned to accommodate visitors.

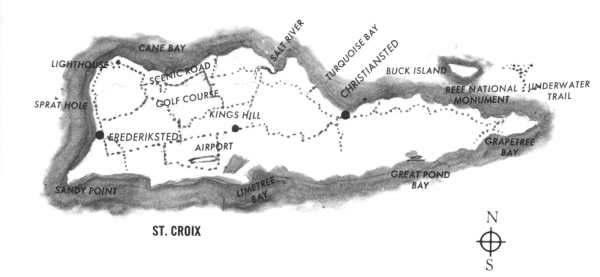

ST. CROIX

N
S

ST. JOHN

It is said that the climate on St. John is so nice that the common cold does not exist there. This island, three miles east of St. Thomas across Pillsbury Sound, is twenty-one square miles in size. The beauty of its green mountains, cool streams, forests, valleys, beaches and sandy bays is astonishing. Coral Bay is one of the best harbors in the Lesser Antilles.

This island, founded by the Danes, had the first slave rebellion in the Caribbean in 1731. The white population was all but exterminated. French forces came in finally to subdue the rebel blacks. Were that not so, St. John might have been the first black republic in the Antilles.

Today this is a beautiful, lonely island, with about 750 native inhabitants and a hundred continentals, mostly retired folks from the mainland United States. The Virgin Islands National Park was created here by a gift to the United States government from Laurance Rockefeller of 5,000 acres. He has also built a resort hotel on St. John, and escapists are arriving in increasing numbers.

Continued on page 52

page 33

OLD SAN JUAN: CASTILLO DE SAN FELIPE DEL MORRO, PUERTO RICO.

This great fortress is the chief tourist attraction of Old San Juan. Built by the Spanish at the northwest end of the city from 1539 to 1586, it covers more than two hundred acres and rises 145 feet above the ocean. The castle was continuously improved until 1787. It is now a National Historic Site.

page 34

FAST-GROWING MODERN SAN JUAN

One of the fastest growing modern cities in the U.S.A. and one of the largest (455,000 population) in the Caribbean islands, San Juan attained its present elegant appearance in less than two decades. The picture shows a small part of the great new city, the Condado section with many new apartment houses and hotels along a beautiful beach.

page 34

OLD SAN JUAN: CITY WALL, SAN JUAN GATE, FORTALEZA

Here are three historical landmarks of Old San Juan. La Fortaleza, the oldest governor's mansion in continuous use in the New World, overlooks the old city walls at the right. San Juan gate to the left, completed in 1641, was once the main entrance to the walled city of San Juan. The massive ramparts and walls of the town are very impressive.

page 35

PUERTO RICO: LUQUILLO BEACH

A few miles east of San Juan is the magnificent popular beach, Luquillo. It ranks among the most beautiful beaches in the world: crescent-shaped covered with fine white sand, surrounded by a forest of coconut palms. The waters are calm, clear, blue-green in color. It is well-kept by the Puerto Rican government.

page 36

TRUNK BAY, ST. JOHN, U.S. VIRGIN ISLANDS

Once the richest of the Virgins, with 109 estates, St. John is today a quiet, secluded island, an escapist's paradise, for most of the early inhabitants died in a slave revolt in 1733. A large part of the island is a National Park. Jungle overgrew the old estates, and today one sees green mountains, sandy bays, deep valleys, sparkling water and white sand beaches. One of the thirty-one bays with a beautiful beach is Trunk Bay, with clear, calm waters, perfect for snorkelers and divers.

page 37

CHRISTIANSTED, ST. CROIX, U.S. VIRGIN ISLANDS

This well-preserved Danish port was for many years capital of the Danish Virgin Islands. With its romantic streets and interesting historical buildings painted in pastel colors, it is one of the highlights of every Caribbean visit.

page 37

BUCK ISLAND REEF NATIONAL MONUMENT, ST. CROIX, U.S. VIRGIN ISLANDS

This island, just off the coast of St. Croix, was designated a National Monument because of the barrier reef that surrounds the eastern part of it. In the

Continued on page 49

SAN JUAN, PUERTO RICO: MORRO CASTLE

33

SAN JUAN: CONDADO SECTION

PUERTO RICO

OLD SAN JUAN: FORTALEZA, SAN JUAN GATE, CITY WALL

PUERTO RICO: LUQUILLO BEACH

U.S. VIRGIN ISLANDS

CHRISTIANSTED

← *TRUNK BAY, ST. JOHN*

UNDERWATER TRAIL, BUCK ISLAND, ST. CROIX

HARBOR OF ST. THOMAS, U.S. VIRGIN ISLANDS

CHARLOTTE AMALIE FROM BLUEBEARD'S CASTLE

ST. THOMAS, U.S. VIRGIN ISLANDS

SAPPHIRE BAY

ROAD TOWN
TORTOLA

BRITISH
VIRGIN
ISLANDS

THE BATHS, VIRGIN GORDA

SABA

IN THE RUINS
OF ORANJESTAD,
ST. EUSTATIUS

41

PHILIPSBURG, CAPITAL OF DUTCH ST. MAARTEN

MULLET BAY EIGHTEEN-HOLE GOLF COURSE, DUTCH ST. MAARTEN

*VIEW OVER
SIMSON BAY
LAGOON AND
FRENCH SIDE
OF ST. MARTIN*

*BEACH, LITTLE
BAY BEACH HOTEL
DUTCH ST. MAARTEN*

ST. MAARTEN
(ST. MARTIN)

*VIEW OVER
GREAT SALT
LAKE TO SABA*

MONTSERRAT: CAPITAL PLYMOUTH WITH SOUFRIERE (3002 FT.)

LOOKING OVER
  ST. CHRISTOPHER (ST. KITTS)

AIR VIEW OF ST. BARTHELEMY (ST. BARTS)

ST. JOHN'S, CAPITAL OF ANTIGUA

ANTIGUA: HISTORICAL ENGLISH HARBOUR →

TYPICAL BEACH, ANTIGUA

SUGAR MILL RUIN

ANTIGUA
COUNTRYSIDE

NATIVES

clear lagoon between the island and the reef are remarkable formations of elk-horn, staghorn and brain coral, with colorful fish and other interesting marine life. Buck Island, just a mile long and about 300 feet high, is easily reached from Christiansted.

page 38
HARBOR OF ST. THOMAS, U.S. VIRGIN ISLANDS

Approaching St. Thomas by air from the northwest, this beautiful view opens into the harbor, with Charlotte Amalie, the capital, in the background. To the right is Water Island.

page 39
CHARLOTTE AMALIE, VIEW FROM BLUEBEARD'S CASTLE, ST. THOMAS, U.S. VIRGIN ISLANDS

One of the great views of St. Thomas: As we look down from the terrace of Bluebeard's Castle, the harbor of St. Thomas and the city of Charlotte Amalie surround us with a unique setting. To the right is Charlotte Amalie; in the background French Town and Water Island. In front is a Royal Poinciana tree in full bloom, a glory of the Caribbean.

page 39
SAPPHIRE BAY, ST. THOMAS, U.S. VIRGIN ISLANDS

One of many beautiful beaches of St. Thomas is at Sapphire Bay, framed by sea grape trees and coconut palms.

page 40
BRITISH VIRGIN ISLANDS

So peaceful, unique and unspoiled in natural beauty are the British Virgin Islands, you are mindful of what the earth might have been like at its creation. Looking down from a plane on Tortola and other British islands, they resemble a dark emerald necklace gleaming in the tropical sun. They are reserved and quiet, ideal for dreamers and people seeking complete relaxation.

page 41
SABA

This imposing volcanic rock rising from the Caribbean is five square miles in size, 2,900 feet in height, and one of the most memorable specks of land in the West Indies. Saba, which is Dutch, has several villages, but no harbor, no sandy beach. There is a landing strip, Yraus-quin Airport, on its northeast corner. There are good accommodations for tourists on the island. The heart of this strangely beautiful island is cool, fresh and green. Mt. Scenery, seen in the photograph, is the highest peak on the island and the highest mountain in the Netherlands Antilles.

page 41
ST. EUSTATIUS (STATIA)

This Dutch island was once the most important trading center in the Caribbean. It was of great assistance to the American Revolution, and from Fort Oranje the first foreign salute to the U.S. flag was fired on November 16, 1776. For this act it was sacked by Great Britain and the capital, Oranjestad, completely destroyed in 1781. There is now an airport, the hotel "Golden Era", and two guest houses on the island. Windward Islands Airways connects it with St. Maarten by a short flight.

page 42

PHILIPSBURG, CAPITAL OF DUTCH ST. MAARTEN

Philipsburg is located on a flat lagoon between the Great Salt Pond (foreground) and Great Bay. It is a small, colorful town with a long history of salt production in nearby Great Salt Pond.

page 42

MULLET BAY, ST. MAARTEN

On the Dutch side of the island along the south coast is a string of magnificent beaches: Little Bay, Great Bay, Simson Bay, Maho Bay. Close to the French border is Mullet Bay, with a beautiful beach, golf course and resort, where this picture was taken.

page 43

VIEW OVER SIMSON BAY LAGOON

This interesting air view over Simson Bay Lagoon, which belongs in the foreground to Dutch St. Maarten, shows in the background Baie de Marigot and the mountains of the French territory of the island.

page 43

ON THE BEACH OF LITTLE BAY BEACH HOTEL

Little Bay offers one of the most beautiful sandy beaches in Dutch St. Maarten. There is the Little Bay Beach Hotel, with more than 100 rooms and an attractive gambling casino. The picture shows the beach with Cay Bay Hill in the background.

page 43

VIEW OVER GREAT SALT POND TO SABA

Looking down from Prince's Quarter Hotel over the Great Salt Pond, there is Philipsburg, the capital of Dutch St. Maarten in the middleground and the outline of the island of Saba visible on the horizon. This tremendous rock in the Caribbean Sea is one of the great attractions near St. Maarten.

page 44

MONTSERRAT: CAPITAL PLYMOUTH WITH SUFFRIERE (3,002 FEET)

Looking from the west to the green mountains of Montserrat, Plymouth, the capital, is in the foreground. This is a lively city with government offices, a few small hotels and good theater, in addition to the usual local entertainment of calypso and steel bands. Montserrat is one of the most beautiful, unspoiled islands of the Caribbean. Covered with green forests with clear streams and waterfalls, it has marvelous drinking water and a plentiful supply of it. When other islands suffer from drought, Montserrat sends shiploads of crystal clear water.

page 45

LOOKING OVER ST. KITTS (ST. CHRISTOPHER)

A view from the ramparts of Brimstone Hill Fort, St. Christopher's mighty fortification, shows in the far distance the silhouette of St. Eustatius and in the foreground the fertile land of St. Kitts.

page 45

AIR VIEW OF ST. BARTHELEMY (ST. BARTS)

The photograph shows the western part of the quaint island and the capital, Gustavia, with the finest harbor in the Caribbean. Measuring only eight square miles, it has a population of about 2,400, mostly descendants of Frenchmen who came to the island in the seventeenth century from Normandy, Brittany and Poitou. The French were the first to colonize St. Barts, but in 1784 they ceded it to Sweden in return for trading rights in Goetheborg. It was returned to France in 1877, but during the period of Swedish rule its capital had acquired the name Gustavia, for Gustavus III, and this is still its name.

page 46

ST. JOHN'S, CAPITAL OF ANTIGUA

This is St. John's, a lively city and capital of the island of Antigua. Located on the northwestern shores of the island, it has an excellent deep water harbor and several good hotels.

page 46

ANTIGUA: BEACHES ARE BEAUTIFUL

Antigua is blessed with some of the best beaches of the West Indies. They are located all around the island in beautiful bays, along peninsulas—along stretches of fine white sand surrounded by coconut palm groves. The picture shows Jolly Beach on the west coast of Antigua.

page 47

ANTIGUA: HISTORICAL ENGLISH HARBOUR

One of the spectacular attractions of Antigua is English Harbour, where Lord Nelson labored to prepare his fleet, which in time destroyed Napoleon's sea-power at Trafalgar. English Harbour, a chain of bays reaching deep into the island, offered a perfect hideaway for the British fleet. As you pass through the dockyard gates you have the impression of stepping into the late eighteenth century; old cannons, anchors, sun dials and caldrons for boiling pitch abound. The entire area is alive with memories of Antigua's exciting and romantic past.

page 48

SUGAR MILL RUIN

It's a typical countryside scene of Antigua: A sugar mill ruin, the native woman with the basket on her head, the children astride the mule could have been photographed anywhere in Antigua.

page 48

NATIVES FROM THE COUNTRYSIDE

These people were photographed at St. John's market, Antigua, where they were offering their merchandise, vegetables, fruit, bread, from their countryside farms.

Continued from page 31

THE BRITISH VIRGINS

Not counting all the little cays, there are about 40 British Virgins, of which only 17 are inhabited. Tortola is the largest with about 9000 inhabitants, next is Virgin Gorda with approximately 1000 people. The islands are mountainous, highest is Sage Mountain (1780 ft.) on Tortola with a beautiful rain forest.

Tranquil is the word for these islands. They embody many Americans' (especially northerners') dream of a serene, remote South Sea island, the dream of a perfect vacation. There are 30 hotels, inns and guest houses with about 1000 beds, the year 'round temperature is between 77°-85°, at night 10-15° less, no really rainy season, last hurricane in 1924. There are about 120 boats for charter with additional 500 beds.

And what great sports and recreation: Unexcelled sailing, fishing (four world records include an 845 lb. Marlin), diving (beautiful coral reefs and plenty of ancient shipwrecks), swimming and tennis. No golf, no T.V., no bigtime entertainment, no noisy jetport. There is spectacular sightseeing, sunning on quiet, isolated white beaches, dancing at the hotels, one movie theater and shopping in Road Town, Tortola, capital of the islands. There is a hospital with 9 doctors and plenty of churches: Catholic, Anglican, Baptist, Methodist, Seventh Day Adventist, Church of God, Jehovahs Witnesses and Pentecostal.

The islands are about 60 miles east of Puerto Rico, 12 miles east of St. Thomas, U.S. Virgin Islands, with excellent flight connections from both.

The total population is a little more than 11,000, under British rule for over 300 years. Currency is the U.S. Dollar.

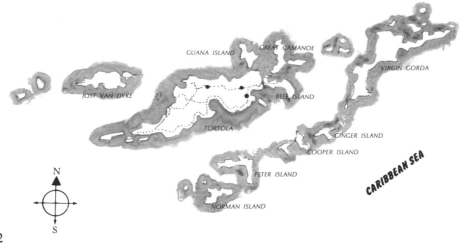

ST. MAARTEN

The visitor to St. Maarten can enjoy two different worlds, and both are delightful. This charming speck of land in the arc of islands that form the Lesser Antilles covers thirty-seven square miles. Of these, sixteen square miles are Dutch and twenty-one are French. The Dutch call their portion of the island Sint Maarten. The French portion is Saint Martin. The people speak English and live in good neighborly fashion without friction. Dutch St. Maarten is a member of the Netherlands Antilles, and Philipsburg is the principal town. French St. Martin is a commune of the department of Guadeloupe, one of France's four overseas departments. Marigot is its principal town. There is no problem going back and forth across the borders of the two sections of this peaceful island.

Columbus gave the island its name in 1493 when he sailed past on his second voyage on November 11, saint's day of St. Martin de Tours. Caribs lived there, and early settlers avoided them. St. Maarten became a harbor of refuge for Dutch vessels in 1620, and the Dutch built a fort. They found salt beds and began the export of salt, an important trade item. The French in 1629 built a small fort on the island. The Spanish reconquered St. Martin in 1633 and built another fort on the heights above Point Blanch.

Peter Stuyvesant, who was later to become the first governor of New Amsterdam, lost his leg here while leading a Dutch attack on the Spaniards in 1644. The Dutch and French returned in 1648 and made a treaty of friendship.

During the next two centuries the flags flying over the island changed sixteen times, and English fleets were continually attacking. Since 1816 the Dutch have had control over their portion of the island.

Today St. Maarten, as a member of the six islands of the Netherlands Antilles, is an equal partner in the Kingdom of the Netherlands. There is universal suffrage. The executive of the Netherlands Windward Islands is the Lieutenant-Governor, appointed by the Queen of the Netherlands. In the French portion of the island the mayor, who is elected by voters, administers St. Martin and St. Barthélemy.

Roads, airports and radio-telephone communications were built in the 1960's with a grant from the Netherlands Government. A drive to court tourists was launched at that time. Tax advantages were designed to increase the building of hotels and new industries. There are no import duties and no excise taxes.

The island today offers numerous delightful and individual hotels, excellent facilities for cruise ships and visiting yachtsmen, splendid restaurants, great beaches with wonderful coral reefs in the surrounding waters, and gambling in continental casinos. More and more visitors are learning that life can be sweet in St. Maarten, and the people are prospering and happy.

ST. EUSTATIUS

Spell it Sint Eustatius and call it Statia. It is a lonely little island, an arid plain between two low mountains. The Quill, 1,800 feet above sea level, is the highest elevation. Today there are about 2,000 inhabitants, many of Indian descent. During the American Revolution 20,000 people lived there and often as many as two hundred sailing ships loaded with arms, ammunition and supplies for the revolutionaries were anchored in the port at Oranjestad. In those days Statia was The Golden Rock.

The visitors who reach this backwater in time may not know or remember that once St. Eustatius was a key port of the Caribbean and the principal base of the great Dutch seafarers of the seventeenth and eighteenth centuries. Franklin D. Roosevelt knew and remembered, and on the island is a plaque sent by that U. S. president in 1939 in gratitude for the help Statia gave to the U.S.A. in winning the war against England. A British admiral in 1781 said, "This Rock, only six miles in length and three in width, has done England more harm than all the arms of her most potent enemies, and alone supported this infamous rebellion."

Statia's stormy past is in great contrast to its quiet life today. Only one of the fine old mansions of the great Dutch traders remains. Almost all of the people are black, and they work hard at farming and raising goats, sheep and cattle. The little island is Dutch, one of the Netherlands Antilles, but everybody speaks English.

SABA

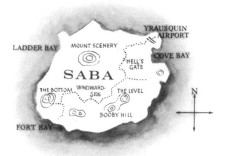

Unique, unforgettable Saba is an extinct volcano rising out of the sea on the edge of the Atlantic in the Lesser Antilles. It has no beaches, no fringing coral reefs. Cloud-wreathed Mount Scenery is the highest peak, 2,900 feet above sea level. It is the smallest of the three windward islands of the Netherlands Antilles. Saba lies twenty-eight miles south of St. Maarten and seventeen miles northeast of St. Eustatius.

The four charming and colorful villages on Saba are Hell's Gate, Windwardside, St. John and The Bottom. The Bottom is the principal village. The name is derived from the Dutch word "botte," which means bowl. The tiny villages of Hell's Gate and Windwardside are perched on the crest of the volcano, and these villages near the top of the mountain are cool and wind-washed. All are quaint, snug places with a Dutch flavor, lushly blooming tropical trees and flowers. There is a hospital, schools, and in each village a small library. The neat cottages have red-shingled roofs, white picket fences and green shutters. The atmosphere is idyllic, peaceful, evocative of a colorful past.

Daily flights from St. Maarten swoop in over the rim of the crater to land on the airstrip. Arriving by sea is even more of an adventure than arriving by air. Ships must anchor in either Fort Bay or Ladder Bay, and passengers are taken to shore in small boats. The road up the steep cliff is winding and narrow, and there are only six miles of road on the little island. The villages have several nice, old-fashioned guest houses, with good, simple food.

ST. BARTHELEMY

They call it St. Barts, and it is a refreshing hide-away in the uppermost corner of the Lesser Antilles, fifteen miles southeast of St. Maarten.

Although the island was first settled by the French and is French today, it was a Swedish colony from 1784 to 1877. The only town on the island is Gustavia, named for a Swedish king.

Volcanic rocks cover the hillsides of the eight square miles of land. Coral reefs and shallows surround the island. There are some magnificent beaches on the north shore. Lobster fishing in the clear waters brings considerable income to the islanders. The people are friendly, frugal and orderly, hospitable to strangers. Most of the natives speak English and French. Many of the men go to sea while the women stay home and weave straw. There are a number of attractive seaside resorts, and the delectable food is French with Caribbean overtones. There is none of the glitter of the larger islands luring tourists, no nightclubs, not even a local radio station.

ST. CHRISTOPHER (ST. KITTS)

St. Christopher has been called St. Kitts since 1623, when the English arrived and settled this island in the northerly leeward group of the Lesser Antilles. It was their first colony in the Caribbean, and became known to the English as the "Mother Colony of the West Indies." Vast fertile plains spread around a volcanic peak. The Carib Indians called St. Kitts, Liaguiga, "the fertile land." Mount Misery is the cloud-capped peak of the central mountain range and rises 4,314 feet. Sugar cane is the principal crop of St. Kitts. Cotton and vegetables are grown on the lower slopes of the mountains. Higher up are lush green forests. The black-sand beaches are of volcanic origin, as are those of many of the neighboring islands.

The most impressive man-made artifact on the island is the massive fortress, Brimstone Hill, built by the British in the eighteenth century. It is a monumental structure, and the view from the top of the 750-foot fort is spectacular, with the horizon rimmed with peaks of the neighboring islands. A winding road on which a car can be driven reaches almost to the top.

St. Kitts was once home to a man who gave his name to the flaming poinciana tree that has become one of the most colorful glories of the Caribbean. He was Phillipe de Langvilliers de Poincy, who ruled the island during twenty-one years of French possession. The remains of the Chateau of M. de Poincy may be seen by making arrangements with the Fountain Estate House.

ANGUILLA

St. Maarten, twelve miles across the Anguilla channel, is the nearest neighbor to Anguilla. Anguilla means "eel" in Spanish, and, indeed, the island does have a serpentine shape. It is a low land with fine beaches, sixteen miles long, and two miles wide.

Fishing is excellent in the surrounding waters, and the islanders are good boatbuilders. Salt has been harvested at Sandy Ground for centuries. Most of the native islanders, however, work in Jamaica, St. Thomas, and other neighboring islands.

NEVIS

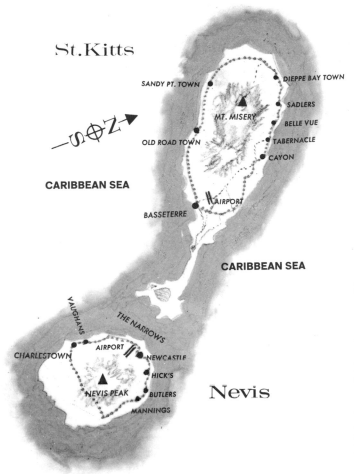

This leisurely, tranquil and beautiful little island was named Nuestra Senora de la Nieves, "Our Lady of the Snows," by Columbus because its mountain, Nevis Peak, is almost always wrapped in white clouds. The small island is eight miles long, six miles wide, and its slopes are covered with greenery, flowers and fruit trees. It is linked to its neighbors in the Leeward Antilles by air service from Antigua and a ferry from St. Kitts. Pinney Beach is a long, golden strand shaded by coconut palms.

Alexander Hamilton was born on Nevis. A young British Captain, Horatio Nelson, was married here to an attractive widow, Frances Nisbet, and a future king of England, Prince Clarence, was his best man. The record of the marriage is in St. John's Church at Fig Tree Village.

Today the majority of the people are black, and they are gracious and hospitable to strangers. Charlestown, the chief village, is small. The first capital, Jamestown, slid into the sea in an earthquake in 1680. There are a few new hotels, an attractive inn perched on a cliff, and other hostelries that were once great plantation homes. Some of the native dishes are a gourmet's delight — pixilated pork, turtle steak, egg plant soup and the roe of sea urchins.

ANTIGUA

Antigua, with Barbuda and Redonda, has full internal self-government in association with Great Britain in independent statehood. The people are predominantly black, the language is English. Agricultural pursuits are on the wane; industry and tourism are on the rise. The 108 square miles of land are fringed by some of the finest beaches in the Caribbean. The soil is fertile, with fields and pastures and low rolling hills. The island is green with native forests and with imported flowering and fruit trees.

St. John's on the northwest coast, is the capital of Antigua. It has an excellent deep water harbor where cruise ships dock. The man-made harbor was completed in 1968 and can accommodate vessels drawing thirty-five feet. St. John's is a bustling port city, with many free-port shops, banks, cinemas and art galleries. St. John's Cathedral, on top of the hill, is beautiful.

On the southern coast, English Harbour and Nelson's Dockyard are delightful attractions, the mecca of yachtsmen. From this base Lord Nelson, then Captain Nelson, sailed against England's foes in the Caribbean. In 1949 English Harbour was a ghost town, abandoned and decaying. In that year the Nicholson family sailed in there to refit, on their way to Australia. There they stayed, and chartered their fine yacht. That was the beginning of the renaissance of English Harbour, today one of the most popular ports for yachtsmen in those seas. The harbor is rimmed by old forts, and is a delightful place to explore.

Visitors can find all they need to enjoy a perfect vacation. There are more than two dozen resort hotels. Everything is at hand for water sports—great beaches, excellent offshore fishing, a good charter fishing fleet, water-skiing, skin-diving, sunken ships to explore off Barbuda, and yachts for charter. Golf courses, tennis courts and duty-free shopping are also among the amusements.

MONTSERRAT

CARIBBEAN SEA

More American retirees have made their homes in Montserrat than in any of the other islands. It is an alluring and salubrious haven, and many attractive retirement homes have been built there. The mountainous cone of land is ribbed by deep green valleys with clear, flowing little mountain streams (called "guts"). There is a feeling of remoteness from hustle-bustle.

Once this was a land of fertile sugar and cotton plantations. When slaves were freed, most white people left. Many black islanders also departed to earn their living in the British Isles, for this was an English colony. Tomatoes, cotton and cattle are the principal crops today. With the influx of Canadians and Americans making their second homes here, there is a new lift in the economy.

The beaches are black volcanic sand, but enjoyable. The energetic explorer can hike up on the mountains through the rain forest and inspect a "soufriere," a hot volcanic sulphur spring. A popular pastime is hunting the giant mountain frog, the "crapaud," a delicacy known as mountain chicken.

There are several hotels in Plymouth, the principal town, and on the cliffs. Saturday is Plymouth's big day, when all the back-country people bring their produce to the town's "Green Market." The Montserrat Yacht Club offers facilities for yachtsmen, and sports include cricket, golf and tennis.

BARBUDA

Barbuda makes an attractive target for a sailing expedition from Antigua. It lies twenty-five miles north of Antigua and is sixty-two square miles in area. Barbuda, once known as Dulcina, is a flat coral island with a large lagoon on the western side. It has miles and miles of pink and white sand beaches. The principal village is Codrington, and there is an attractive hotel there. A small air strip is nearby. The population is little more than a thousand, and most of the people make their living by fishing and catching lobster. Barbuda is a sportsman's paradise, for deer, wild pig, guinea fowl, pigeons and ducks are plentiful.

GUADELOUPE

Guadeloupe rises from the sea in the arc of the Lesser Antilles, five hundred miles from Caracas, Venezuela, and 310 miles from Puerto Rico. It is really twin islands that resemble in shape the two wings of a butterfly. Together they cover an area of about 690 square miles. They are separated by a natural channel, the Rivière Salée (Salt River). A bridge spans the mangrove-fringed channel.

The western island, Basse-Terre, also called "Guadeloupe proprement dite," is a rugged and hilly country. One peak reaches 4,900 feet. Grand-Terre, the eastern of the twin islands, is flat and fertile. The languages spoken on Guadeloupe are French and a Creole dialect.

Columbus discovered this land on his second voyage. Carib Indians living there called the island "Karukera" (Island of Beautiful Waters). Beautiful indeed are the waterfalls that come from so high up that they seem to fall from out of the sky. The Caribs discouraged the Spanish attempts to colonize Guadeloupe for more than a hundred years, and the Spaniards gave up trying to settle there in 1604.

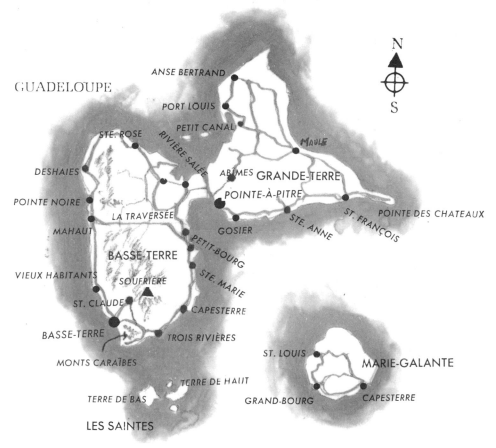

GUADELOUPE

The French were the first to successfully settle the island in 1635, with L'Olive and DuPlessis as leaders. For more than two centuries the European powers fought over the beautiful island. The English made many attacks and gained control in the Seven Years War (1759-1766). After giving up Guadeloupe to the French, the English again captured the island in 1794, were driven out, held it again, and then discontinued the fighting. Since 1816 France has held Guadeloupe. Today it is an incorporated department of the Republic of France and its people have equal rights with the citizens of France.

Point-à-Pitre is the chief port and flourishing commercial center of Guadeloupe. It lies at the southern end of the Rivière Salée on Grande-Terre and gives an impression of a miniature, tropical Paris. On the other end of the mountainous island is Basse Terre, the attractive capital city. Banana boats on the long pier, a seventeenth century cathedral, handsome residences and a huge old fortress, St. Charles, are among the interesting aspects of the capital.

Continued on page 84

Descriptions of the following pictures

page 65
POINTE DES CHATEAUX, EAST END OF GUADELOUPE
One of the more spectacular views in the Caribbean is the east end of Guadeloupe (Grand-Terre), Pointe des Châteaux, with its picturesque rock formations. Great waves break against these dark rocks, and the clouds are driven swiftly by the steady trade winds. A good auto road leads from St. François to the point where this picture was taken.

page 66
VIEW FROM GOSIER TO BASSE-TERRE, GUADELOUPE
A beautiful scene opens from Gosier over the ocean to Basse-Terre and its high mountains covered with dense tropical rain forests. Visible in the foreground is part of the fine beach around Gosier.

page 66
GUADELOUPE: TERRE DE HAUT, LES SAINTES
Off the southeastern coast of Basse-Terre and facing the town of Trois Rivières is the island group Les Saintes, which can be reached by boat or plane from Guadeloupe. It is a group of five hilly islands with several villages and beautiful scenery. Terre de Haut and Terre de Bas are the important ones. The picture shows Terre de Haut, with residents of Breton and Norman descent who, with few exceptions, are fishermen. Just outside of Terre de Haut on Ilet à Cabrit is a first rate hotel, "Fort Josephine." It has a main house with bungalows and is a paradise for sports fishermen.

page 67
ROSEAU, CAPITAL OF DOMINICA
Surrounded by the high mountains of Dominica, Roseau is a town of about 15,000 inhabitants, still quite primitive, and with one good hotel, "Fort Young." The beauty of the island lies inland, in the high green mountains, the tropical vegetation, the streams and waterfalls, the plantations and the Carib Indian Reservation.

page 67
DOMINICA: CARIB INDIAN WOMAN
Deep in the mountains of Dominica but close to the coast is the Carib Indian Reservation, with about 1,500 inhabitants. It is governed by the Carib Council and a chief, who is now elected every three years. Their features are Asian and their skins reddish brown. They rarely mix with other races. Their main settlement, Salybia, has a school building and a Catholic church. Most of the Indians are Catholics.

page 68
HISTORICAL DIAMOND ROCK
One of the great historical landmarks on the south coast of Martinique, it figured in the war between Napoleon France and England in 1804. For more details see page 88.

page 68
FORT-DE-FRANCE, CAPITAL OF MARTINIQUE
Superbly located on an excellent harbor, the capital is surrounded by hills and faces a wide bay beside the Caribbean Sea.

Continued on page 81

POINTE DES CHATEAUX, EAST END OF GUADELOUPE

GUADELOUPE

TERRE DE HAUT
LES SAINTES

ROSEAU, CAPITAL OF DOMINICA

DOMINICA

CARIB INDIAN WOMAN

*HISTORICAL
DIAMOND ROCK*

MARTINIQUE

*FORT-DE-FRANCE
CAPITAL OF MARTINIQUE*

SOUTH COAST
WITH
MT. LARCHER

MARTINIQUE

ST. PIERRE WITH MT. PELÉ

ST. LUCIA: PETIT PITON, A LANDMARK OF THE CARIBBEAN

CASTRIES AND HARBOR

ST. LUCIA

PIGEON ISLAND FROM REDUIT BEACH

COUNTRYSIDE　　　BARBADOS　　　*IN BRIDGETOWN*

BARBADOS

CARIBBEAN COAST AT ST. JAMES

CODRINGTON COLLEGE

PARADISE BEACH AT FRESHWATER BAY

TOBAGO, AN EXOTIC ISLAND

COLORFUL FISH, CORAL,
GORGONIANS AND SPONGES

IN THE CLEAR WARM WATERS
OF THE CARIBBEAN SEA

STRIPED PORK FISH AND CORAL

TRINIDAD

CARNIVAL

STEEL BAND AND LIMBO DANCERS

MOSQUE IN ST. JOSEPH

EAST INDIANS IN TRINIDAD

TRINIDAD

OLDEST BOTANICAL GARDEN IN THE NEW WORLD

ST. VINCENT

BANANA

LOADING

78

ST. VINCENT: DEEP WATER HARBOR OF KINGSTOWN

CARRIACOU, GRENADINES

OVER THE GRENADINES

PALM ISLAND

page 69
MARTINIQUE: SOUTH COAST WITH MT. LARCHER

The southwest end of Martinique is dominated by Mt. Larcher. The picture was taken near Diamant, looking west along the southern coast.

page 69
MARTINIQUE: ST. PIERRE WITH MOUNT PELE

Along the entire western coast from the town of Schoelcher to the town of St. Pierre there are excellent beaches with fine grayish sand, a permanent reminder of the volcanic activity of Mount Pelé, which broods in the background. In 1902 St. Pierre was a lovely city of more than 30,000 inhabitants when it was totally destroyed by an eruption of Mount Pelé. Today the ruins tell the story not only of a fantastic disaster but also the great past of a town once called "Pearl of the Caribbean."

page 70
ST. LUCIA: THE PITONS

The two picturesque mountain peaks behind the schooner are the Pitons— Gros Piton and Petit Piton — rising sharply from the Caribbean Sea to heights of 2619 feet and 2,461 feet respectively. Clearly outlined against the sky, they are outstanding landmarks of the Caribbean islands.

page 71
ST. LUCIA: CASTRIES AND HARBOR

Flanked by two hills Castries, the capital of St. Lucia, has one of the loveliest and safest harbors and best yacht anchorages in the Caribbean. It is a favorite port of call for cruise ships. Only a few minutes from town is beautiful Vigie Beach, with a strand of white sand that stretches for more than three miles.

ST. LUCIA: PIGEON ISLAND FROM REDUIT BEACH

Reduit Beach on the northwest coast of St. Lucia is one of the best beaches of St. Lucia. Two elegant resorts are located there. In the background is Pigeon Island, connected by a causeway with the main island.

page 72
BARBADOS: HISTORICAL CAREENAGE

One of the landmarks of Barbados is this colorful inlet at Bridgetown, capital of the island. There are busy wharves where, for more than 300 years, ships of all makes and origins have docked for overhauling, cleaning and caulking. The scene is changing fast, old buildings are being replaced with new and modern ones, and in a few years it will all be very different. This is one of the most picturesque points in Barbados. In the background visible is St. Michael's Cathedral, built in 1665, rebuilt in 1789.

page 72
BARBADOS: COUNTRYSIDE

Hills with sugar cane fields and bananas, ancient greathouses of estates, sugar mill ruins, churches with old grave yards, palms, frangipani and casuarina trees—that's the countryside of Barbados. George Washington loved it. He wrote that he was "perfectly enraptured with the beautiful prospects . . . on every side the fields of cane, corn, fruit trees in a delightful green setting."

page 73
BARBADOS: CARIBBEAN COAST
The beautiful beaches in St. James Parish along the Caribbean Sea are called the Platinum Coast of Barbados. Some of the best resorts of Barbados are in this neighborhood: Sandy Lane, Coral Reef, Miramar, Colony Club and others. Sailing, fishing, water skiing, diving, snorkeling and boating are some of the many sports offered to the tourist here.

page 73
CODRINGTON COLLEGE
Christopher Codrington founder of this seminary, was born in Barbados in 1668. In 1700 he became governor of the Leeward Islands, retiring to Barbados in 1707, where he died on Good Friday, April 7, 1710. He left his two sugar estates to the Society for the Propagation of the Gospel in London, to be used for the founding of a college for the study of religion and medicine, under vows of chastity, poverty and obedience on the lines of a monastic order. Anglican priests of the Community of the Resurrection in Mirfield (Yorkshire) keep up this work in affiliation with the University of Durham (England).

page 73
PARADISE BEACH AT FRESHWATER BAY, BARBADOS
Stretches in front of an attractive resort not far from the capital Bridgetown tall casuarinas trees frame the magnificent beach.

page 74
TOBAGO AN EXOTIC ISLAND
Can you imagine Robinson Crusoe in these surroundings? Tobagonians believe that Daniel Defoe had their romantic tropical island in mind when he created his masterpiece. Here are many small, sandy beaches set in coves or half-moon bays. The visitor succumbs easily to Tobago's sundrenched attractions, the outstanding tropical vegetation, and particularly the exotic birds living here.

page 75
IN THE CLEAR, WARM WATERS OF THE CARIBBEAN SEA
A wonderland of exotic life, brilliant colors and unusual forms is revealed to the diver and snorkeler around the Caribbean islands. Colorful fish, coral, gorgonians, sponges and molluscs live in the reef formations surrounding most of the islands. Some are well known, such as the Buccoo Reef at Tobago, the Buck Island Reef National Monument at St. Croix, the Sea Gardens at Barbados and the reefs surrounding Grand Cayman. But there are so many more. One of the finest sea gardens at Tobago lies just outside of Arnos Vale on the northwestern coast of Tobago. Beautiful formations are around Antigua, and the reefs about the Grenadines are outstanding for their variety of sea life.

page 76
TRINIDAD: CARNIVAL
In all the world there is no carnival celebration to equal Trinidad's annual madness. Fantastic costumes, individual or worn by stylized groups, wild, noisy or harmonious music—these mark a spontaneous celebration climaxed with organized parades and shows on the Savannah and in Independence Square in Port-of-Spain. During this two-day delirium of sight and sound (Monday and Tuesday before Ash Wednesday) the streets of Port-of-Spain are overflowing with jubilant people jumping

and stamping to the tunes and rhythms of steel bands and calypso groups. Our picture shows a typical street scene, alive with the carnival atmosphere.

page 76
TRINIDAD: STEEL BAND AND LIMBO DANCERS

The Caribbean's popularity all over the world during the last two decades must be credited in part to calypso, the steel band and the limbo, a form of dance which developed from an old African ritual of manhood. All three evolved and became formalized in Trinidad, and today can be heard and seen all over the West Indies and in the night-clubs of the United States, Canada and Europe. Oil drums are the major instrument of a typical steel band, while the limbo dancer attempts to "clear" under a bamboo bar as low as ten inches from the ground.

page 77
TRINIDAD: MOSQUE IN ST. JOSEPH

This is one of the many attractive mosques for the Muslim population of Trinidad. There are approximately 50,-000 followers of the teachings of the Prophet Mohammed on the island.

page 77
TRINIDAD: EAST INDIANS IN TRINIDAD

More than 300,000 East Indians comprise a large part of Trinidad's total population. These people, particularly the older ones, adhere strictly to their own customs and religion, colorfully expressed in their traditional garments, foods and in many small homes which are scattered all over Trinidad.

page 78
ST. VINCENT: OLDEST BOTANICAL GARDEN IN THE NEW WORLD

More than 200 years old, this garden has a fine selection of tropical trees, including descendants of the original breadfruit seedlings brought to St. Vincent by Captain Bligh from Tahiti on his post-Bounty voyage in the Providence.

page 78
ST. VINCENT: BANANA LOADING

It is a colorful picture in the harbor, when the peasant women bring the harvest of their banana fields, well packed and carried on their heads, to the banana boat.

page 79
ST. VINCENT: DEEP WATER HARBOR OF KINGSTOWN

The modern deep water harbor of Kingstown invites many cruise ships to St. Vincent. It was also important to improve the harbor a few years ago because of the export of the island's agricultural produce. Agriculture is the basis of St. Vincent's economy and provides more than two thirds of the total employment. The principal products are bananas, arrowroot, nutmeg, yams, coconut, cassava and sea island cotton. Kingstown is an impressive city, with its colorful gardens, stately churches, government buildings and attractive harbor.

page 80
CARRIACOU, GRENADINES

Located on the southern end of this small island chain, Carriacou is the largest island (13 square miles) of the Grenadines. It is a beautiful island with green mountains surrounded by a wonderfully clear sea with many interesting reefs perfect for diving and snorkeling. There are several attractive settlements with Hillsborough the largest one. The island has a good airfield, many good roads, a hospital and a good place to stay, the Mermaid Tavern.

page 80
PALM ISLAND, GRENADINES
About 125 peaks of an underwater mountain range rising out of the sea be-tween St. Vincent and Grenada—these are the Grenadines. They range greatly in size and topography. Around the islands are large coral reef formations, which are visible in this view of Palm Island, a small, well-cultivated island east of Union. It has an airstrip with frequent flights scheduled from Grenada, St. Lucia and St. Vincent. It also has an attractive resort on a beautiful beach and good anchorage nearby.

continued from page 63

From Basse-Terre a fine auto road leads along the coast, with unspoiled scenery and beautiful beaches. Arrangements can be made in that city for cars and guides for a fascinating excursion to the top of a dormant volcano, Sufrière. The road leads through a magnificent rain forest and the refreshing waters of natural hot springs are found along the roadside. Another enjoyable drive on Guadeloupe is the trip over the mountain on a new auto road, La Traversée. It leads through wild jungles and dense rain forests. Many charming and interesting villages and beautiful beaches are found throughout the twin islands. A stirring view that enchants artists and photographers is the sight of the surf breaking on huge rocks at Pointe des Chateaux on the east point of the island.

LES SAINTES

Small, green and hilly are Les Saintes, Guadeloupe's five little neighbors. Terre de Bas and Terre de Haut are the principal islands, linked to Guadeloupe by ferry and airplane. Though they are idyllically remote, there is an excellent new hotel at Ilet á Cabrit just outside Terre de Haut. This is a sports fisherman's haven.

The natives of the islands are intriguing. Most of the population of Terre de Bas is black. The majority of residents of Terre de Haut is white, descended from sea-faring Bretons and Normans who settled there long ago. Many still make their living today by fishing.

The men wear quaint hats, unique among the islands. It is woven of straw and bamboo, shaped like a parasol and is about a foot and a half in diameter. It is covered with a white fabric and attached to the top of a cylinder that fits tightly on the head. The hat, called a "salaco," resembles those worn by Chinese coolies.

DOMINICA

Dominica looks today very much as it did when Columbus first sighted this dramatically beautiful island on his second voyage in 1493. On it today still live some of the descendants of the Carib Indians who successfully discouraged settlement for a long time. It is the northernmost of the Windward Islands, and lies thirty miles south of Guadeloupe. The mountainous, green-clad country is a land of running waters. There are said to be 365 rivers, which have carved deep valleys and gullies. Dominica is twenty-nine miles long and sixteen miles wide, rugged in terrain and mostly undeveloped.

The highest peak is Morne Diablotin, which rises 4,747 feet and is covered with forests of mahogany, cedar and bamboo. For those who enjoy a feeling of isolation, and for the adventurous and hardy explorer, Dominica is perfect.

Roseau, the capital, is perched on the slopes. It is the island's principal settlement, rather than Portsmouth on the coast, which was once malarial. The malaria has been eradicated and the Dominicans hope to make the town a tourist development. The Botanical Gardens at Roseau are among the most interesting in the Caribbean. Nearby are twin waterfalls, Layou and Pagoua, romantic with their flying spray. Morne Valley is the home of Rose's Lime Juice. There are several hotels in Roseau and on a nearby silky black beach. There are also guest houses at the Archbold Plantation.

The magnificent back country of Dominica is for those energetic souls who do not mind hiking along paths through fern-filled rain forests. The Twentieth Century has left the people in the mountain villages almost untouched. The Transinsular Road offers breathtaking scenery.

On the eastern coast is the Carib Reserve, where about 1,500 people of Carib blood live around a village called Salybia. Although their blood has been mixed and their language is English, they are Indian in feature. They are lively, keen-eyed and prideful. Bananas are the Caribs' principal source of income. The men build dugout canoes and the women weave baskets. There is a road to the Carib Reserve.

MARTINIQUE

Martinique strikes the observer as having the kind of natural beauty that would inspire Gauguin. In fact, it did. Paul Gauguin painted there before he wandered on to Tahiti.

The women possess a beauty that has turned the heads of emperors. A creole lady born at Trois Ilets became the Empress of France—Josephine Bonaparte. Napoleon remarked, "I hold Martinique dear for more reasons than one." Another lady from Martinique, Francoise d'Aubigne, became Madame de Maintenon, second wife of King Louis XIV. Perhaps the most romantic bride of all was Aimée du Buc de Rivery. Born on Martinique, she attended a school in France. On the way back to her island home, the ship on which she sailed was captured by Barbary pirates. She was taken to the Grand Turk in Istanbul and made to join his harem. Soon she became Sultana, and eventually the mother of Emperor Mahmoud II.

Martinique and its people still inspire love at first sight. It is the largest and most northern of the Windward Islands, and is French in a unique way. The island contains 425 square miles of land and 345,000 people live there. The people are free and equal citizens of France. In 1946 the island became a department of France, with a prefect and all the rights and privileges of metropolitan France. The social legislation, a model for the rest of the Caribbean, provides social security, allowances to large families, and free medical care for the needy. There is little illiteracy because of the excellent primary school system throughout the island, and about ninety-five per cent of the children attend school.

Martinique is framed in magnificent blooms and tropical forests. The Carib Indians were impressed by the flowers and called the island Madinina, "Island of Flowers."

The French were the first settlers on the island in 1635, and they fought over Martinique with the British for years. The island is French today because Louis

XV preferred the West Indies to Canada, and swapped the latter for the former at the Treaty of Paris in 1763.

There were two major cities on Martinique on May 7, 1902. They were St. Pierre and Fort-de-France. Then the volcano Mt. Pelé exploded the next day and destroyed St. Pierre. Thirty thousand people died in one of the worst natural disasters in history. Today the ruins of that city are the Pompeii of the Caribbean.

The capital of Martinique and the French West Indies is Fort-de-France, the quintessence of France with a Caribbean flavor. There is a fine harbor, with Fort St. Louis on one side, a green park in the center, and yellow buildings and sidewalk cafes on the other. Flowing through the town are two rivers—Rivière Madame on the north and Rivière Monsieur on the south. The balconies and the lacy iron grill-work of the city are reminiscent of old New Orleans.

An historical landmark is Diamond Rock on the south coast of Martinique. On January 7, 1804 the British occupied the Rock with 110 sailors for about 17 months disturbing with their cannons the French navy to move in this important passage. Only on June 29, 1805 they gave up to the French in a highly dramatic encounter.

ST. LUCIA

St. Lucia, for long a sleeping beauty, is now waking up and enchanting tourists. This island is endowed with great beaches and splendid mountain scenery, plus good harbors. It is 238 square miles in size. The people, who are predominantly black, speak English and French. These is an English governmental heritage and a French cultural heritage. It is an independent state in association with Great Britain.

The Island was first discovered by Columbus in 1502. Caribs drove off the first Englishmen attempting settlement. The French made the first successful settlement in 1650, and thereafter St. Lucia changed hands between the British and the French fourteen times. Legacies of that fighting are forts on Morne Fortune and Vigie Hill. The island became a British colony in 1814, and is self-governing today.

Castries, the capital and major city, has a fine deep water harbor, often filled with large ships and sailing vessels. It was built after a great fire in 1948.

St. Lucia is unique in that it has a drive-in volcano, La Soufrière. It is possible to drive a car almost to the edge of the crater of this steaming, active volcano, and to walk down and watch the waters bubble and steam. Sulphur baths nearby have been used for centuries, and are famous for their curative qualities.

Two of the most outstanding landmarks of the Caribbean are St. Lucia's twin peaks, Gros Piton and Petit Piton. These spectacular spires rise straight from the sea on the leeward coast. They have been a landmark to navigators for centuries. Their steep forested sides are a challenge to experienced mountain climbers.

The Pitons are near the town of Soufrière, which is St. Lucia's second largest city, fifteen miles south of Castries on the coast. It has an attractive French colonial flavor. Diamond Bath nearby offers health baths in hot mineral springs, which are found frequently in the area.

Among the great beaches of the island is Vigie Beach, three miles of snow-white sand bathed by gin-clear water near Castries. On the northern shore is Reduit Beach, with Pigeon Island about a mile offshore connected by a causeway.

South of Castries is Marigot Bay, fine small anchorage for yachts. The sheltered bay has a green-clad shore, clear water for snorkeling, a yacht club and hotel. Beyond the town of Vieux Fort on the southern end of the land is Anse de Sables, one of the finest beaches on the island. It is sheltered from the Atlantic surf by off-shore coral reefs.

BARBADOS

Barbados has been beloved by sun-seekers for several centuries. Indeed, George Washington slept here, when he brought his brother, Lawrence, to the island to recuperate from tuberculosis. Barbados is the only land outside North America on which Washington ever set foot. One of the island's charming hotels dates back to 1878, and is still in operation. Many elegant resorts and tourist accommodations have been added since then.

This small island has a quiet, cultivated countryside that suggests southern England transplanted to the tropics. It has always been British, and its Old World charm is British to the core. Combine an eighteenth century atmosphere with a benign climate, many miles of white sand beaches, interesting villages in rolling hills and you have the secret of Barbados.

Good, though narrow, roads encircle the island and crisscross through the hills. The east coast on the Atlantic, and the west coast on the Caribbean are equally attractive, but quite different. On the Atlantic coast is Sam Lord's Castle, a splendid plantation house built in 1830. Today it is an elegant resort with a beautiful beach.

The shores become steeper to the north and here the Atlantic pounds the rocks with huge breakers. Bathsheba is the home of the Flying Fish Fleet, and it is also an attractive windward resort. From the village of Tent Bay nearby the brightly painted fleet sets out almost every day to net flying fish, which are considered the tastiest treat Barbados has to offer. They are practically the emblem of the island.

The western, leeward coast of Barbados is sheltered from the pounding surf. It is known as the "platinum coast," the Riviera of Barbados. Both shores have magnificent, soft, white sand beaches, but the clear Caribbean is far gentler than the Atlantic. On this side of the island is Speightstown, the second largest city on Barbados. The center of the elegant and exclusive resort area is St. James. The western shore contains a variety of accommodations, ranging from modest to luxurious resorts. North of Bridgetown on the western shore there are more than a dozen superb resorts, and there are equally as many to the south of the capital. There is a social cachet to wintering in Barbados that keeps these resorts nicely filled.

Sports are dear to Barbadians. Cricket is their favorite game, and some native players enjoy fame throughout the cricket-playing world. From July through December is the season for polo-playing. The horse-loving British have also seen to it that there is first-rate horse racing at Garrison Savannah. Islanders and visitors find that the rolling country with its beautiful views of the sea is perfect for exploration on horseback. There are three golf courses on the island and numerous tennis courts. Football, basketball and netball are also popular. Every kind of water sport can be enjoyed. The clear, quiet waters of the west and southern coast are sheltered by coral reefs, and offer fine underwater sightseeing. Fishing is good especially from February to May when the migrating schools pass by. Small boats can be rented; yachts chartered.

ST. VINCENT

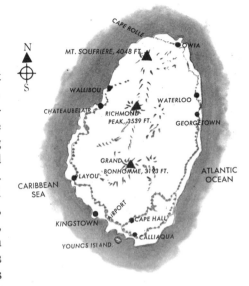

St. Vincent has the reputation of being the most cheerful and festive of the Windward Islands. Among its other distinctions is that it exports millions of tons of arrowroot starch each year to the United States, and it has a breadfruit tree growing in Kingstown's Botanical Gardens from a seed brought back by Captain Bligh from Tahiti. St. Vincent is said to resemble Tahiti. It is a beautiful island eighteen miles long and eleven miles wide, with palm-lined beaches and good roads. Rivers, streams and waterfalls lace the forested mountain slopes. The volcano, Soufrière, 4,000 feet high, is the highest peak and a blue lake is cupped in its cloud-shrouded crater.

The Caribs called this island Haroun, "Land of the Blessed." St. Vincent and Dominica are the only two islands in the West Indies where one can meet Caribs today. This is indeed a melting pot. The English, the French, and the Caribs alternated in fighting one another. The English finally won. The language is English, but many of the people are of French descent. In addition there are Black Caribs, Africans, Portuguese and East Indians.

Green hills rise behind the red roofs of Kingstown, the principal city. St. Vincent's Botanical Gardens are the oldest in the Caribbean. It was the poverty of St. Vincent that caused the British Crown to send Captain Bligh on the Bounty to bring back breadfruit, which is a staple food. From Kingstown there is a road that winds eight hundred feet up to the ruins of Fort Charlotte. This was built by the British in the early years of the nineteenth century, and offers a fine view over the city to the sea.

South of Kingstown is Caliaqua, an attractive area with nice beaches. Just offshore is tiny Young Island with fine beaches beneath rocky cliffs. Here is an elegant resort hidden away in the tropical vegetation. The neat grounds are pastoral, and there is a delightful pool overhung with flowers and ferns.

THE GRENADINES

There are hundreds of Grenadines, if rocks and reefs are included. However there are only about 125 islands strung out along this chain throughout seventy miles of the Caribbean between St. Vincent and Grenada that are large enough to deserve the name. On these dots of land, the peaks of volcanic mountains emerging from the sea, live some fourteen thousand people, and most make their living from the sea. Only ten of the islands have a permanent population. They are truly outposts of civilization. All are English in government. Most of them are associated with St. Vincent. Grenada administers a few of the islets and Carriacou at the southern end of the string. The inhabitants speak English.

Bequia, northernmost of the group, is nine miles south of St. Vincent. On this island Admiralty Harbor is a safe, sheltered anchorage, and the village facing the harbor, Port Elizabeth, is delightful. Soft white beaches stretch away on all sides, and Princess Margaret Beach is one of the prettiest in the Caribbean. The village consists of a few small inns, a few small stores, a few churches, and a small hospital. The atmosphere is idyllic.

South of Bequia are little unoccupied islets—Battowia, Petit Nevis, Baleceaux, Quartre. Next comes Mustique, which is being developed as a private and exclusive resort. The next large island is Cannouan, which has good harbors at Grand Bay and Charles Bay. Then come the Tiny Tobago Cays, and Mayreau, a larger island with high hills and a few hundred inhabitants.

Union Island's thousand foot mountain is a landmark. There is a road here that climbs to an old French fort, good anchorages, and inns in the village of Clifton. Palm Island, once Prune Island, is being developed by an American as an attractive cottage-resort. It has an airstrip with frequent scheduled flights. Petit St. Vincent is a small, civilized island with a handsome inn, guest cottages and boats for sailing and fishing. The largest island in the Grenadines is Carriacou which has miles of good roads, an airfield and an attractive inn.

GRENADA

Grenada has mountains mantled in green, lush tropical valleys, magnificent beaches, and a leisurely, sweet atmosphere. It also has a race track, good roads, excellent resort accommodations, art galleries, golf courses, tennis courts and movies. The island has absorbed these elements of civilization in a delightful fashion.

Grenada is known as the "Spice Island of the West," and the air is fragrant with the smell of cinnamon, vanilla, ginger, mayberry and nutmeg. Almost a third of the world's spices are grown here. St. George, the port and chief city, is one of the most delightful little towns in the Caribbean. This toylike town sits on a hill beside the excellent harbor. Pastel-painted, red-roofed houses have outer staircases, fan-shaped windows and wrought-iron balconies. Though Grenada is one of the British Windward Islands, it has a French flavor.

Grand Anse Beach, one of the finest in the Caribbean, is about a mile from St. George. Excellent hotels rise beside the shining sand along this two-mile beach. Among the other pleasant places to visit are the colorful markettowns of Grenville and Goyave, the beaches at Pointe Saline, Levera Beach, and the pretty homes at Westerhall Point, a narrow peninsula where eight hundred poinciana trees have been planted. Halifax Harbour is a snug inlet that offers shelter to boatmen in storms, and has a nice beach inn.

The Dougaldston Estate near Charlotte Town is fascinating. Charlotte Town is a shipping center for spices, stored in ancient stone buildings. At the Dougaldston Estate the visitor can see nutmegs, allspice, cloves, black pepper, cinnamon, touca beans, bay leaves, vanilla and cocoa beans growing and being processed.

The mountainous interior of the island is as delightful as the shore line. Roads and paths lead into a dramatic landscape, complete with waterfalls, orchids, and an occasional funny little monkey. A road leads to the top of Grand Etang, a volcanic crater with a lake in the crater. Paths through lovely woodlands filled with flowers wind round to Annandale Falls.

93

For more ambitious mountain climbers there is Mount St. Catherine, the highest peak on the island and Mt. Qua Qua. Julien Fedón, a mulatto planter who led a bloody rebellion against the English, made his headquarters on Mt. Qua Qua. It was also here he finally surrendered. Near the town of Sauteurs the Indians who first lived on Grenada threw themselves into the sea when threatened with capture by the French.

TRINIDAD

Southernmost of the Caribbean islands, Trinidad is only sixteen miles off the coast of Venezuela. The mountainous island has peaks more than 3,000 feet above sea level, and seven lovely rivers that keep the fertile land green with forests and farms. Pitch Lake, one of the largest asphalt lakes in the world, is a peerless phenomenon that covers one hundred acres and is nearly three hundred feet deep. Asphalt from this lake covers the highways of the world.

When Columbus discovered Trinidad on his third voyage he found Arawaks living here in settled villages making music with drums and conch shell horns. In 1592 the first permanent settlement was established by Spaniards in the town of St. Joseph on the Caroni River. It was later sacked by Sir Walter Raleigh. The French from Haiti and other French islands moved in by the thousands in 1780, the year of the slaves' revolution in Haiti, at the invitation of Spain's King Charles III. The British captured the island in 1797, and British it remained thereafter. In 1962 it became an independent nation within the British Commonwealth.

Trinidad gave the world the steel band. They are direct descendants of the voodoo drums of Africa. These unique bands evolved from the "Tamboo-Bamboo" Carnivals, which for years fostered the native musical skill of the African islanders. Musicians beat rhythms by knocking together pieces of bamboo, while merrymakers chanted tunes. Today the steel drums have been fairly well standardized. They range from full-sized forty-four gallon oil drums to the Ping Pong, a drum cut to about six inches from the top.

The island is also recognized as the home of calypso, the folk songs of Afro-West Indian. Calypso is poetry and song, witty and satirical. It serves as town crier and village gossip as well as rich entertainment.

Today Trinidad is the most industrialized and wealthiest island in the Caribbean. Sugar cane, cocoa, rice, bananas, citrus fruits, copra and many forest products are exported. Asphalt is a major export, and the island is today the second largest source

Map of Trinidad showing: VENEZUELA, Maracas Bay, BLANCHISSEUSE, TOCO, Galera Point, ATLANTIC OCEAN, St. Joseph, Northern Range, ARIMA, PORT OF SPAIN, VALENCIA, Matura Bay, PIARCO, Airport, CHAGUANAS, COUVA, Central Range, Cocos Bay, GULF OF PARIA, RIO CLARO, SAN FERNANDO, PRINCES TOWN, Mayaro Bay, LA BREA, Pitch Lake, FYZABAD, Oil Wells, TRINIDAD. Compass rose marked N, S.

of oil in the British Commonwealth, with a large Texaco refinery near San Fernando. Trinidad also has a good supply of natural gas. Chemical industries, a modern soap factory and a paint plant are among the many industries that have in recent years located in Trinidad. They have been lured there both by the availability of industrial fuel and by special tax concessions designed to encourage local and foreign investment. In the last decade large sums have been spent to improve harbors, roads, bridges, water supply, land drainage and reclamation, electricity production and housing.

The island is mountainous in its northern range, which extends from east to west. In the center are the Montserrat Hills and in the south the Trinity Hills. The rest of the country is fertile flat land.

There are excellent hotels and resort accommodations in Port-of-Spain, the capital, and nearby Maraval and on some of the island's superb beaches. Almost all of the

continued on page 116

95

Descriptions of the following pictures

page 97
GRENADA: THE HARBOR OF ST. GEORGE'S
Grenada is one of the most beautiful scenic islands of the West Indies. Its capital, St. George's, is situated on a craggy peninsula spectacularly colorful, with red-and-white houses, green hills and the azure waters of the harbor. Its streets are almost medievally narrow and twisting. Government offices now occupy Fort George, which was built in 1705 by the French. Just south of the city is Grand Anse, Grenada's famous beach.

page 98
CURACAO: NATIVE SINGERS AND MUSICIANS
The people of Curaçao cultivate the traditions of their island, wearing old custumes, and preserving traditional music and dances. The couple on the left is a member of a folklore group of singers and dancers who perform from time to time in the city. The musicans to the right use some of the old traditional instruments of the island.

page 98
CURACAO: BREEDESTRAAT, BUSINESS STREET IN WILLEMSTAD
Breedestraat is the elegant shopping street in Willemstad, capital of the island. The building to the left, with the bells, is the home of Spritzer & Fuhrmann, famous jeweller of Curaçao. Many fine stores are on this street: Penha, Wooden Shoe, Kan Jewelers, Van Dorp, Casa Amarilla, El Globo, New Amsterdam Store, Salas and others. The street has a colorful line of old Dutch houses interspersed with modern structures which harmonize with the old ones.

page 99
CURACAO: WESTPOINT, BEACH AND TOWN
Far to the west of the island is the village of Westpoint, which has a nice beach on the leeward coast.

page 99
WILLEMSTAD, CAPITAL OF CURACAO
Uniquely Dutch and definitely European is the city of Willemstad. The picture shows some of the ancient fortifications with the waterfort to the right. This fortress has been converted into a modern hotel of imposing dimensions,

page 100
ARUBA: THE HARBOR OF ORANJESTAD (PAARDEN BAY)
Oranjestad is the capital and largest town on the island. It is situated on the leeward coast and has a fine natural deep-water harbor. The port of Oranjestad is the commercial harbor of Aruba well-protected by a coral reef and open day and night. The picture shows the town of Oranjestad in the background.

page 100
CARNIVAL IN ARUBA
Carnival in Aruba is a great event for all three ABC islands. Traditionally it takes place on the last three days before Ash Wednesday. Thousands of onlookers fill the streets, windows and balco-

Continued on page 113

THE HARBOR OF ST. GEORGES, GRENADA

NATIVE SINGERS AND MUSICIANS

CURACAO
BREEDESTRAAT, WILLEMSTAD

WESTPOINT, BEACH AND TOWN (CURAÇAO)

WILLEMSTAD, CAPITAL OF CURACAO

HARBOR OF ORANJESTAD
(PAARDEN BAY)

CARNIVAL IN
ORANJESTAD

ARUBA

THE FAMOUS BEACH

ARUBA   COVE AT ANDICOURI

COUNTRYSIDE WITH DIVI-DIVI TREE, HOOIBERG AND BOULDER FORMATIONS

BONAIRE

SECLUDED BEACH

BONAIRE'S FLAMINGO COLONY

PORT ANTONIO

JAMAICA

RAFTING ON RIO GRANDE

CALYPSO SINGERS

JAMAICA

DUNN'S RIVER FALLS →

DRAMATIC ART

THE SEVEN MILE BEACH

GRAND CAYMAN ISLAND

GEORGE TOWN, CAPITAL OF THE CAYMAN ISLANDS

GRAND CAYMAN WRECKS AT THE REEF

CAYMAN BRACK: THE BLUFF

RUINS OF SANS SOUCI-
PALACE AT MILOT

HAITI

← THE WATERFALLS
OF SAUT D'EAU

HAITI'S FAMOUS
PRIMITIVE ARTISTS

←

ALCAZAR DE COLON (1510)

TOMB OF CHRISTOPHER COLUMBUS

SANTO DOMINGO, DOMINICAN REPUBLIC

nies to watch the procession of marchers garbed in colorful customes and masks parading through Oranjestad. Many visitors come from Curaçao, Bonaire and Venezuela.

page 101
ARUBA: THE FAMOUS BEACH

On the sheltered western coast of Aruba, where there are luxurious resort hotels; the island is fringed by what seems to be an unending beach of snow-white sand. One beach follows the other, on and on. Among the most beautiful is Palm Beach, where this picture was taken.

page 101
COVE AT ANDICOURI, ARUBA

One of the most inviting coves on the wave-battered north coast of Aruba is the one at Andicouri, with its small sandy beach and picturesque rock formations. This is a favorite place with Arubans for outings, picnicking and fishing. Wading into the rushing waters is a delightful pastime.

page 101
COUNTRYSIDE OF ARUBA, WITH DIVI-DIVI TREE AND HOOIBERG.

Two symbols of Aruba are the Hooiberg (Haystack Mountain), visible from all over the western part of the island, and the divi-divi tree in the foreground. The divi-divi trees are shaped by the northeast trade winds, that air condition the island naturally. The tree grows straight up from the ground for about seven to nine feet, and then the crown streams out horizontally to the southwest, blown always by the prevailing wind.

page 102
BONAIRE: FLAMINGO COLONY

Bonaire, second largest of the ABC islands (Aruba, Bonaire, Curaçao), has one impressive attraction of which no other island in the Caribbean can boast. Huge flocks of flamingos breed in the island's great salt lake. Thousands of them wade and fly around the lake, a splendid sight especially fascinating to bird watchers.

page 102
BONAIRE: ONE OF THE MANY SECLUDED BEACHES

Bonaire is an escape island with only a few hotels. There are beautiful secluded beaches (see picture), good sailing and fishing and very interesting bird watching. In addition to the famous flamingo colony there are many other interesting birds—snipes, sandpipers, war-birds, white and blue herons, ducks, pintails, pelicans, some parrots and many more varieties.

page 103
JAMAICA: PORT ANTONIO

This is Jamaica—high mountains, lush green vegetation, good harbors, palm-framed beaches, friendly villages, and, all around, the clear, blue waters of the Caribbean Sea. The photograph depicts one of the loveliest areas of Jamaica, a section of the northeast coast. Here, nature has been at her most lavish and beautiful vistas abound. The view shows the twin harbors of Port Antonio, with the town on the peninsula separating the two bays.

← *CARIBBEAN MOON NIGHT*

Continued from page 95

beaches are accessible by good roads. Port-of-Spain is a fascinating city to explore, and is especially exciting at carnival time. Here there are mosques, Victorian mansions, and other architectural structures and styles in the private homes on the Savannah, which is the two hundred acre Central Park of the city. The Savannah is the setting for the festive carnivals.

Cricket, a favorite sport in Trinidad, is played in Queen's Park Oval, which can hold thirty thousand spectators. St. Andrews Golf Course, founded in 1890, is world famous. It is at Maraval and has two eighteen-hole courses. There is a nine-hole course at La Brea. There are three horse-racing tracks—at Port-of-Spain, San Fernando and Arima. Small game is hunted on the island, which is well stocked with deer, wild hog, alligators, mongooses, and certain game birds.

TOBAGO

Tobago is a simple island, with natural beauty and an unsophisticated charm. This mountainous island has good beaches, beautiful views, doll-like villages and the golden-feathered Greater Bird of Paradise. This is the last stand of that rare and magnificent bird. Tobago is also said to be the legendary home of Robinson Crusoe and his man Friday, and Crusoe's cave is said to be located on a most beautiful and desolate beach.

Tobago was not always as peaceful as it is today. It changed hands thirty-one times. The Spaniards who settled nearby Trinidad ignored it. The Dutch, the French, the English, natives of the Duchy of Courland (now Latvia), and pirates fought over it. At one time in the eighteenth century it was agreed that Tobago would remain a no-man's land, and pirates moved in for a while. The English first settled on Tobago in 1763 and planted sugar cane. It became an English possession in 1803. Tobago was a ward of Trinidad until, along with Trinidad, it became in 1962 an independent member of the British Commonwealth.

Scarborough, the capital, is on the southeastern shore facing the Atlantic, and most of the hotels are on that side of the island. The quaint town fronts on Rockly Bay and is backed by hills. North of Scarborough on the windward coast are pleasant little fishing villages—Mount St. George, Pembroke, Roxborough, Delaford and Speyside. Two small islands lie offshore from Speyside, and the bigger is called Little

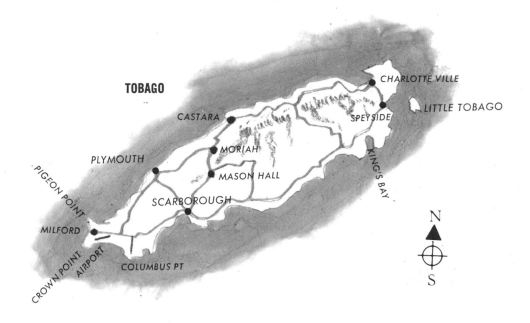

TOBAGO

CHARLOTTE VILLE
LITTLE TOBAGO
CASTARA
SPEYSIDE
PLYMOUTH
MORIAH
KING'S BAY
MASON HALL
SCARBOROUGH
MILFORD
N
CROWN POINT AIRPORT
PIGEON POINT
COLUMBUS PT
S

Tobago or Bird of Paradise Island. It was to this island that Sir William Ingram in 1912 brought the Birds of Paradise that were originally native to the Aru Islands of New Guinea, where they were threatened with extinction by plume hunters. He gave Little Tobago to the Government as a permanent sanctuary.

The road curves across the hills in the northern part of the island to Charlottesville, which has a good beach, and then follows the coast south to Plymouth and Crown Point. There are fine beaches on the Caribbean side at Store Bay, Great Courland Bay and Buccoo.

Tobago's Buccoo Reef off the southwest coast is one of the most beautiful coral reefs in the Caribbean. There are fish-filled coral canyons exotic in design, in warm, crystal-clear water that tempt the snorkeler to hang above them for hours. There are also evidences of old ship-wrecks, which conjure up the possibilities of pirate treasures under the sands.

☆

MARGARITA

For those who have dreamed of pearl-diving in pellucid waters, Margarita is the island. A fortune has been brought up in pearl oysters from the sea around Margarita. This is a Spanish island, in language and culture, linked to Venezuela by ferry and by an aqueduct that brings water from Cumana on the mainland. It is also linked by government.

It is as much fun to explore the land of Margarita as it is the water around it. Small colonial Spanish villages, fertile valleys, flocks of scarlet ibis along the waterways, ancient churches, beautiful beaches tempt the adventurer to wander about.

The principal town is Porlamar, near the airport. This is a vivid, colorful town, especially at carnival time in February, and from May through September, when there are music and folkloré festivals, yacht regattas, and fiestas. Christmas here is celebrated with traditional and wonderful bird and fish dances.

The roads round the island are good, passing beside a peaceful beach at El Morro, through a fishing village, Bella Vista, and Pampatar, with its colonial church. The capital town is La Asunción, north of Porlamar. Founded in 1562, it is an attractive Spanish colonial city with a great Cathedral, a museum, the Government palace, ruins of ancient buildings and a palm-lined square.

Several dozen pleasant hotels are scattered about Margarita. The beaches and the skin diving could not be better. Cockfighting is a favorite local sport. The food is wonderful, the fishing fine. Margarita is distinctive and delightful.

CURAÇAO

Gabled seventeenth century Dutch houses, painted in every pastel shade, give the visitor who arrives in Curaçao's capital city, Willemstad, a feeling that he is stepping into a tale by Hans Christian Andersen. This feeling of being a part of a happy fairy-tale persists as he comes to know the island.

Curaçao had a sleepy existence until 1914. The Dutch settled Curaçao in 1634.

Oil was discovered in Venezuela in 1914, and the following year the Royal Dutch Shell Company began to build one of the world's largest oil refineries on the island. Curaçao was off and running and became one of the major commercial ports in the Caribbean.

In the 1950s the government launched a program to encourage tourism in order to give full employment to the citizenry. A luxurious hotel was built into the massive old seaside fort at Willemstad. The ramparts of the fort became a promenade for the guests. Tourists came, fell in love with the island, and many more resort hotels have been built with equal success. Curaçao is one of the most prosperous islands in the Caribbean today.

It is the largest island in the Netherlands Antilles, forty miles from Venezuela. Willemstad is the seat of government of the Dutch islands, active partners of Holland.

In Willemstad the Queen Emma Bridge, across St. Anna Bay, links the two parts of the city, Punda and Otrobanda. It swings open frequently during the day, causing pedestrians to scramble and automobiles to wait. A stroll across this pontoon bridge offers an excellent view of the colorful houses on the waterfront. The fairy-tale feeling persists in the fascinating "Floating Market," schooners loaded with fruits, vegetables and fabrics tied up in a canal beside the harbor.

CURACAO

The Mikve Israel Synagogue, close to the Floating Market, is the oldest synagogue in the Western Hemisphere, dating back to 1732. Beth Haim, the Jewish cemetery west of the city, was consecrated in 1659 and is possibly the oldest Caucasian burial place still in use in the Western Hemisphere. Among the first settlers were Jews who were fleeing the Spanish and Portuguese Inquisitions. They contributed greatly to the economic and cultural growth of the community.

Among the interesting historical buildings is the Old Dutch Reformed Church, rebuilt in 1796 within Fort Amsterdam. There is a fascinating museum in Willemstad with primitive artifacts and interesting historical material.

A ride through the countryside leads to excellent beaches on the leeward side of the island at Knip Bay, Piscadera Bay, Spanish Water, Santa Marta, Santa Cruz and Westpoint. A visit to the Hato Caves is fun. The caves have stalactites and stalagmites. They look like the kind of caves where primitive men might have painted on the walls. Here, however, modern man has done wall murals and the paintings are all lighted in a gaudy, jolly fashion.

The island's low import duties result in bargain shopping for luxury items from all over the world. Curaçao's bargains are famous among knowledgeable travellers. There is excellent jet service and many modern cruise ships make Willemstad a port-of-call.

ARUBA

In huge bat-filled caves on the north coast of Aruba the first settlers left hieroglyphs painted in red dye on the cool cave walls. These first settlers were the Caribs. They gave trouble to the Arawaks who also lived on the island and left pottery as their relics.

It might almost be said that Aruba is that happy land that has no history. The island became a Dutch colony in 1634. Pirates attacked now and then, and a fort had to be built to keep them off. England seized and held the little island from 1805 to 1816, when it reverted to the Dutch. But the scene on Aruba for centuries was largely quiet and peaceful.

For a long time Aruba was a breeding ground for horses. In 1825 alluvial gold was found, but there was little of it. The cultivation of the aloe was promoted to alleviate the lack of industry and other feasible crops in the nineteenth century. Phosphate was mined at the southeast end of the island from 1874 until 1915, when mining ceased because the product couldn't compete on the international market.

Aruba is a serene and peaceful land today, but the economy changed dramatically for the better in the 1920s. Today it is one of the most prosperous and progressive islands in the Caribbean, with a high standard of living. Royal Dutch Shell built a small refinery on the island in 1924. Lago Oil and Transport Company, later purchased by Standard Oil of New Jersey, built one of the largest refineries in the world there in 1927. They refine Venezuelan oil. Lago has boosted the economy both by creating jobs and by being the island's largest taxpayer.

The economy received another big boost in 1958 when the government launched a program to attract tourists and investments. Because the beaches are beautiful, the climate is perfect and the people of Aruba are both gentle and competent, this program has been outstandingly successful.

Though it rarely rains, the cool, silken trade winds air-condition the land. They not only blow dust and insects away, they blow so hard that the divi-divi trees all slant in the direction away from the prevailing wind. These distinctive trees are almost a trademark of Aruba.

As fast as new hotels are built on Aruba, their rooms are filled. Palm Beach, with its miles of white sand, is one of the most beautiful beaches in the Caribbean. There are numerous superb restaurants on the island. Casinos supply night-time excitement. Top entertainers come here for shows. Jet service is convenient.

Oranjestad, the capital city, is a pastel Caribbean version of a little Dutch town, and it is pleasant to walk the clean and friendly streets. The deep harbor often has cruise ships at anchor. Freeport prices in excellent stores make shopping for everything from cameras to porcelain a favorite pursuit of visitors.

Success has not spoiled Aruba. This island is still serene, a land of happy people and soothing beauty.

BONAIRE

Bonaire is enormously appealing, especially to skin-divers and bird-lovers. Here thousands of flamingos mate and nest annually. They feed in shallow lagoons at both ends of the island, especially at Great Salt Lake on the southern side. The road to the lake passes old slave huts and salt pans where slaves once harvested salt. In addition to the dramatically beautiful flamingos there are thousands of green parrots, parakeets, warbirds, herons, terns, pelicans and other tropical species.

The waters round Bonaire are just as rewarding to skin-divers and spearfishermen. International spearfishing tournaments have been held here. There is a big land-locked bay, called the Lac, that is ideal for spearfishing. The island has great white sand beaches, and beachcombers can enjoy collecting conchs. Spiny lobster are found in the shallow waters along the coast, and a fine variety of game fish may be caught or speared offshore.

The capital is Kralendijk, Dutch for "Coral Dike." It is a quaint little spic-and-span Dutch town in the Caribbean style. Sailing vessels come into the small harbor for the fish market on the docks, and this is a pleasant place to stroll and inspect their catches. Kralendijk is on the western coast of the island. Opposite the town is Little Bonaire, a small uninhabited islet that is a pleasant picnic spot for sailing parties.

This tranquil island has good roads from end to end, an airport, and excellent hotel accommodations. It also has a gambling casino, part of recent government efforts to lure tourists. The hotels are on wide, white beaches and have water sports facilities.

JAMAICA

Jamaica, with 4,400 square miles of land, is not only one of the larger islands of the world, it is also one of the most varied in its charms. It has been described as a continent in miniature. White sand shores give place to lush green vegetation, which changes as the observer goes from the low-lands to the alpine heights. Third largest of the Caribbean islands, it is 144 miles long, fifty miles wide.

Columbus came ashore on Jamaica in 1494 on his second adventure in the New World. He named the island Santiago and claimed it for Spain. He made his landing at a beautiful bay on the north coast which he called Gloria.

The Spanish began to settle the island in 1509, when Juan de Esquivel arrived as the first Spanish governor. They established a colony that raised cattle, pigs, sheep, oranges, bananas and other crops. They enslaved the Arawaks, who promptly died, and then brought in the first slaves from Africa about 1517. Initially the principal city was Sevilla Nueva (New Seville), on the north coast. Later the Spaniards moved their main settlement to the southern coast where they built a new headquarters, Santiago de la Vega (St. James of the Plain). Today that settlement, which lies west of Kingston, is known as Spanish Town.

The Spaniards made little effort to develop Jamaica. English privateers and pirates of all nations raided the island. In 1655 an English force on an expedition ordered by the Lord Protector of England, Oliver Cromwell, took Kingston Harbour and the Spanish surrendered. Though the Spanish continued a long guerrilla war against the British from the mountains, Jamaica became a British colony. Runaway Bay on the north coast was the departure point of the last resisting Spaniard, Don Arnaldo de Ysassi, who fled in 1660.

African slaves fought beside the Spanish during those years, and it was then that the Maroon colony of freed Africans was established in the mountains. English settlers and a small colony of Jews immigrated to the island during the latter years of the seventeenth century, and the Maroons continued to live on in the mountains in isolated freedom. They regularly raided the English colonies on the plains. After years of proving that the English colonists could not conquer them and their guerilla bands, the Maroons in 1739 signed a treaty with the British which gave them tax-free land and self-rule. The treaty is still in force today, and the Maroons live peaceably and industriously in their mountain homes.

As sugar cane grew in importance, Jamaica grew in wealth. Planters with money to build sugar mills arrived, and imported African slaves to do the work. There were 10,000 white people and 130,000 slaves on the island in 1750. Britain established a legislative system and built forts to protect what was becoming a rich prize.

Pirates and buccaneers, who were condoned by the authorities, made Port Royal their headquarters, and it became "the wealthiest and wickedest city on the face of the earth." Legends of raids still abound. Port Royal was shaken by an earthquake in 1692 and slid into the sea.

The last half of the eighteenth century was the era of the great sugar-producing estates in Jamaica. There were numerous slave revolutions, until the slave trade was abolished in 1838 and modern Jamaica was born. In fact that year many ex-slaves left the estates and became farmers in their own hill villages. East Indians were brought in to till the fields as indentured laborers between 1845 and 1917. Chinese also immigrated and became shopkeepers, and the Lebanese who arrived at the end of the nineteenth century became successful merchants.

Sunshine and calypso, rafting down a river, sophisticated resorts, theater, sports, dancing, fishing and native cabaret shows—the entertainment offered to vacationers in Jamaica is delightful and varied. The mountainous island has five distinctly different resort areas, all linked by good roads.

Kingston on the southern coast is the capital city and the heart of the island's life. Among the many delightful spots to visit around Kingston are the world-famous Royal Botanical Gardens, the historical remains in Port Royal and Spanish Town, the museum and gallery at the Institute of Jamaica, and the attractive University of the West Indies at the foothills of the Blue Mountains.

Port Antonio, beside the sea on the northeast coast, is a mecca for fishermen and offers rafting on the beautiful Rio Grande. Here the Jamaica International Fishing Tournament is held each autumn. The Blue Lagoon is a center of recreation.

Jamaica

ABOLITION OF SLAVERY IN JAMAICA.

PROCESSION of the BAPTIST CHURCH and CONGREGATION in SPANISH-TOWN under the Pastoral care of THE REV^d J.M PHILLIPPO, with about 2000 Children of their Schools and their Teachers, to the Government House on the 1st August 1838, when they were received by His Excellency the Governor SIR LIONEL SMITH who after addressing them, read to them the PROCLAMATION of FREEDOM, amidst the hearty rejoicing of not less than 8000 persons, the majority of whom had previously attended Divine Worship, and also subsequently retired to their respective homes peaceful and happy. — The Governor — The Revd J.M Phillippo and the Bishop are seen standing in front of the Prelate thus representing the happy Union of Civil & Religious feeling on this joyful occasion.

Abolition of Slavery in Jamaica: Spanish Town, August 1st 1838

Ocho Rios, one of the oldest areas of the island, lies on the north coast, and has interesting remains of the early days of Spanish colonization. Here the Spaniards first landed at Discovery Bay, and left from Runaway Bay. Nearby are two spectacular waterfalls, at Fern Gully and Dunn's River.

Montego Bay on the northwest shore is the sophisticated and famed winter resort area. The luxurious hotels with their entertainment, splendid white sand beaches at Doctor's Cave, and clear green waters draw many visitors.

Mandeville lies 2000 ft. above sea level in the cool and lofty central hills of the island, and is a peaceful and picturesque resort. Known as Jamaica's "English village," its stimulating climate and leisurely pace attract vacationers.

Visitors are also lured to Jamaica by all sorts of water sports, championship golf courses and horse-racing at Caymanas Park in Kingston. Yachtsmen find excellent facilities. Tourism is one of the island's major industries, and Jamaica has plenty of natural and man-made attractions.

125

CAYMAN ISLANDS

The three Cayman Islands comprise a dependent territory of Great Britain that rises from the sea in the Caribbean beside the Windward Passage south of Cuba. They do not have to boast to the outside world of their diverse charms, because their loving visitors do.

Nature and wise people who have lived here have blessed them with unusual attractions. Nature gave them one of the most beautiful beaches in the world, Seven Mile Beach on the western side of Grand Cayman. Nature gave them warm, clear water around them, magnificent coral reefs and fish-filled sounds and nearby depths. There was a great sea crop of delectable green turtles and fish to be harvested.

The people themselves, by some blessed alchemy, have become among the friendliest in the world. They came to harvest the sea. Turtling, fishing and salvaging wrecks made them brave. White men had black slaves back yonder. Today more than half the people are a mixture of black and white. There simply isn't any racial strife.

After the pirates stopped coming there and shooting people they didn't like, nobody put anybody else down. There wasn't enough wealth on the islands for anybody to get prissy or biggity. There wasn't much beside the sea to support the early settlers. They caught turtles and fish. They salvaged wrecks on the reefs. They cut mahogany and shipped it to Jamaica.

They got churches first, and then schools, and then good schools. They got roads, with two World Wars slowing them down in physical improvements. Then, in the 1960s and 1970s they got the idea that they didn't want to be one of Great Britain's semi-rebellious colonies in the West Indies, because they didn't have anything to rebel against. They had had benign neglect, plus a fort or two to protect them and that is what they had wanted.

So the voters on these three little islands, numbering a few thousand, voted to secede, as it were, from their relation as part of Jamaica and become a dependent territory of Great Britain on their own.

And then they became what they are today, one of the great tax havens of the world. The Cayman Islands passed laws that are good to money invested there. Some of the very rich of the Western World put their money in Caymanian banks today rather than in Swiss banks. There are 193 banks in George Town, capital of the Cayman Islands.

These islands have become especially appealing to people from North America — people that range from the rich to divers. Caymanians speak English with a Welsh lilt that is touching to the heart. International affairs of the islands are handled by Great Britain, through the Governor. The Cayman laws regarding taxation couldn't be better. Investors, courted by these laws, have built splendid accommodations for visitors — luxurious hotels and apartments. (There are modest quarters, too.) Jets fly in daily. Everybody gets happier all the time in the Cayman Islands.

CUBA

La República de Cuba includes not only the island of Cuba but also the Isle of Pines, a smaller island just south of the western end of Cuba. There are also numerous small cays and islands. The long, narrow island stretches 760 miles from east to west and is twenty-five to 125 miles in width. It lies ninety miles south of the Florida Keys.

This is a green and flowering land with sheltered bays and cliffs along the north coast, where the mountains drop sharply into the sea. The southern coast is low and swampy. There are splendid stretches of white sand beaches. The fertile fields of the western and central section produce sugar cane and tobacco, and cattle ranching is found on less fertile land in the east central part, especially in the province of Camagüey. Pico de Turquino, the highest peak, rises 6,562 feet in the rugged Oriente province. Short rivers run to the sea, and the 150-mile Cauto River is the longest river. The isle of Pines is hilly, well-wooded.

Columbus sighted the island on October 27, 1492, on his first voyage, and he landed on the north coast. He thought he had found Japan or China, though he named the land Juana, for the King of Spain. Later the name was changed to Santiago, and then to Ave María, until finally the original Indian name was restored.

Under a liberal Spanish constitutional government and with Spanish Governors who had a light hand on the reins, Cuba thrived in the late eighteenth and early nineteenth centuries. Then came a series of heavy-handed military tyrants from Spain

CUBA

and discontent flared into civil revolution in 1868. Reforms followed. Slavery was abolished in 1886 and in 1893 blacks and whites were given equal civil status. José Martí led the final fight for independence, which began in 1895 and ended on December 10, 1898, after the U.S. entered the war.

Politically the Negro has been the white man's equal throughout the twentieth century. Spanish slave laws were always comparatively generous and there is almost no color caste on the island.

The majority of workers are engaged in agriculture, fishing and mining, though industry is increasing. The principal crops are sugar, tobacco, coffee and livestock—cattle, pigs and poultry. Cocoa, pineapples, vegetables and rice are also important crops. Tractors have been imported in recent years and the use of fertilizers has increased. Chief exports of Cuba today are sugar, tobacco, coffee, rum and molasses. The surrounding waters are rich in fish, which constitute an important part of the Cuban diet, and there is a large fishing fleet.

HAITI

Exciting, vivid in its beauty, Haiti, the first black republic in the Caribbean, is a land like nowhere else on earth. It is a unique mixture of African and French culture, full of exotic contrasts. Here visitors can enjoy cock-fighting, hunting, gambling, art collecting, nightclubbing, golfing, fishing, undersea exploring and mountain-climbing in surroundings graced with a natural grandeur.

Haiti takes its name from the Arawak word "Hayti," which means The Mountain Country. It occupies the western one-third of the island of Hispaniola with the Dominican Republic on the eastern two-thirds of the island. The Haitians are descended from slaves who came from the Congo, the Gold Coast, Sudan and Senegal, and their blood is laced with that of French plantation owners. The Spaniards came to Hispaniola first, but it had no gold, and they did not do much in the way of settlement in the western part of the island. In the seventeenth century France settled what they called St. Domingue and imported so many slaves that the white Frenchmen were soon out-numbered by more than ten to one.

The great uprising in Haiti came in the midst of the French Revolution. Blacks rose up against mulattoes and their white masters. Toussaint L'Ouverture, Jean Jacques Dessalines and King Henri Christophe were the great black leaders in Haiti's war of independence. Since then the political history of the country has been stormy, but Haiti has been free of foreign rulers.

Hispaniola is the most mountainous island of the Caribbean, and the peaks of Haiti reach to 9,000 feet. The steep land has a network of trails, paths and rough roads leading through rugged beauty. Parts of the country are still largely unexplored.

Port-au-Prince is the capital of Haiti. It combines narrow streets in its old sections with broad boulevards in the newer parts of town. Peasants driving donkeys come in to sell fruits and tourists are driven about in limousines. Massive colonial buildings shelter shops that sell a wide array of imported luxuries to tourists, but the most exciting objects for sale are the primitive paintings and the polished wood carvings. They speak the universal tongue of art with an accent that is uniquely Haitian. Among the interesting places to visit in Port-au-Prince is the National Museum, which has many historical exhibits. They include the anchor of Columbus' flagship, the Santa Maria, which sank off Hispaniola on the first voyage.

Cap-Haïtien, which is called Le Cap, is the second largest city in the country. King Henri Christophe had the royal palace of Sans Souci built for himself here as a Versailles of the New World. The palace, now in ruins, had spacious galleries, panelled rooms, mirrored walls, splendid paintings and 365 doors. It also had a non-electric air-conditioning system.

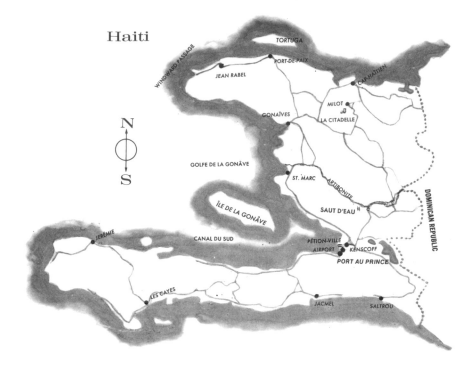

Haiti

The most exciting man-made structure in Haiti is the breathtaking fortress La Citadelle, built by Henri Christophe. It is an imprégnable fortress high in the mountains near Cap Haïtien, reached only by a rough trail. There is nothing like it in the Caribbean. It is built on the scale of ancient Egyptian and Roman monuments to kings and gods. Christophe built it to house ten thousand troops. The walls are twelve feet thick at the base, 140 feet high. The stones are huge. Twenty thousand ex-slaves died in its building. It is a monument to mighty architectural engineering, and to mighty dreams that haunt the rúin. If there were nothing else, a visit to La Citadelle is worth a trip to Haiti.

But there is so much else. There are the ruins of Pauline Bonaparté's castle at Cap Haïtien. There is voodoo. Many of the voodoo rites about Port-au-Prince are staged for tourists, but true voodoo lives in Haiti. It is an African religion in which themes of the Catholic church are interwoven. It is primitive, symbolic, with drums, dancing, wild gyrations, walking through fire, sacrifice of animals. There are, however, no crucifixions. Cock-fights, too, are a bloody aspect of Haitian recreation. They draw gamblers who glory in a contest between two birds that will fight until the death rattle.

The International Casino in Port-au-Prince offers gaming in the continental manner. The island has excellent resort hotels that offer fine food, dancing and sophisticated entertainment. The rewards for those who visit and explore this vivid country are rich memories of an exciting land.

DOMINICAN REPUBLIC

The Dominican Republic, on the eastern two-thirds of the island called Hispaniola, is the land that Columbus loved best, and anybody can see why. High, majestic mountains rise behind the principal city, Santo Domingo. The valleys and the plains are fertile, and support sugar cane, bananas and cattle, horse ranches and mahogany forests. The beaches are beautiful, the clear waters filled with fish and lobster. The flavor of life is Spanish.

Columbus sighted the island on his first voyage in 1492. The Admiral's brother, Bartolomé, settled the capital, Santo Domingo, in 1496. It is the oldest city in the New World. Here Columbus, who died in Spain, was re-buried. His bones lie in the great Cathedral of Santa Maria la Menor in a splendid marble sepulcher. His son, Diego, built his fortress home here. It is called the Alcázar and is a colonial architectural gem, carefully restored and rebuilt. While it was being built Diego Columbus lived in the House of Cord. That house, which dates back to 1502, is the oldest house in the Western World.

Santo Domingo has fine resort hotels. A modern highway takes visitors to the countryside and to popular resorts. Santo Domingo, which is on the south shore, is an elegant capital, with wide and beautiful boulevards, fine homes, lovely parks, a huge outdoor theater and a casino.

In addition to the tomb of Columbus, the magnificent Cathedral of Santa Maria de Menor has some splendid treasures of colonial Spain, including a fortune in jewels, paintings by Murillo and silver by Cellini. It is one of the finest relics of colonial times in the Caribbean, and is lovingly preserved. Numerous other colonial churches are

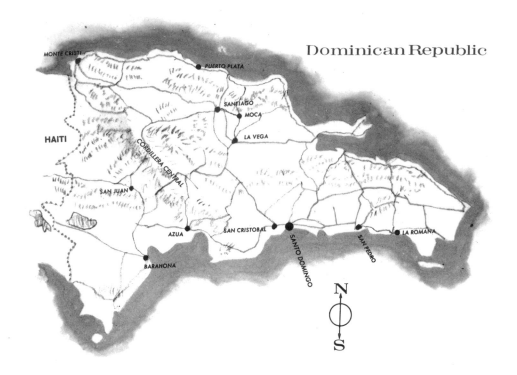

Dominican Republic

equally cherished. Pre-Colombian Indian artifacts and carvings are displayed in the National Museum. The museum itself was once the stables and servants' quarters of Diego Columbus.

One of the most delightful resorts is Boca Chica, twenty miles from Santo Domingo on a four-lane highway. It has a charming inn, fine food and a great beach beside a lagoon. Fishing villages fringe the coast. There is an excellent beach at Guayacanes.

Exploration of the mountains is a great adventure, for they are filled with rushing rivers, waterfalls, splendid woodlands. Santiago and La Vega are two of the attractive mountain towns with good accommodations for travellers.

ACKNOWLEDGMENTS

In the preparation of this book I had the valuable
cooperation of Jane Wood Reno, my son Michael
Hannau and Wim ter Hart. Hedy Eibuschutz did the
fine map for the end paper, my wife Ilse the final
layout of this book. Some material from my
previous books on the Caribbean, which were prepared
with the assistance of others, was used. My sincere
appreciation goes to all who contributed to this volume.

Hans W. Hannau

Alphabetical Index of the Islands

Cuba

Isle of Pines

Cayman Islands

Jamaica →

Hispaniol

Tortuga

Haiti

Dominican Republic

The Islands of the Caribbean

Caribbean

Hedy Eibuschutz

Panama

Colombia